# EASY PICKINGS™
# DYLAN

AMSCO PUBLICATIONS
part of The Music Sales Group
New York / London / Paris / Sydney / Copenhagen / Berlin / Madrid / Tokyo

T0061397

This book © Copyright 2008 Amsco Publications,
A Division of Music Sales Corporation, New York

Exclusive Distributors:
MUSIC SALES CORPORATION
257 Park Avenue South
New York, NY 10010, USA
MUSIC SALES LIMITED
Distribution Centre, Newmarket Road,
Bury St Edmunds, Suffolk IP33 3YB, England
MUSIC SALES PTY LIMITED
20 Resolution Drive,
Caringbah, NSW 2229, Australia

Order No. AM993982
ISBN 978-0-8256-3640-0

Music edited by Tom Farncombe
Music arranged by David Weston
Music processed by Paul Ewers Music Design
Cover design by Fresh Lemon
Cover illustration courtesy iStockphoto
Interior photos courtesy iStockphoto and LFI
Printed in the United States of America

Your Guarantee of Quality
As publishers, we strive to produce every book to the highest
commercial standards. This book has been carefully designed to
minimize awkward page turns and to make playing from it a
real pleasure. Particular care has been given to specifying acid-
free, neutral-sized paper made from pulps which have not been
elemental chlorine bleached. This pulp is from farmed
sustainable forests and was produced with special regard for the
environment. Throughout, the printing and binding have been
planned to ensure a sturdy, attractive publication which should
give years of enjoyment. If your copy fails to meet our high
standards, please inform us and we will gladly replace it.

www.musicsales.com

# WELCOME TO EASY PICKINGS™!

EASY PICKINGS™ is the new way to play classic songs in the fingerpicking style. The music in this book doesn't use standard notation. Instead, a simple system shows the guitar strings.

Chord boxes show you where to place your fingers with your fretting hand; crosses on the strings show you the pattern to pick the strings. That's all there is to it!

All the songs in this book have been specially arranged in the EASY PICKINGS™ format to make them as easy as possible. The first few songs have only a few chords, and simple picking patterns; later in the book the songs have more chords and a greater variety of fingerpicking styles. Some of the songs have been arranged in a different key from the original recording. Where this is the case, you'll need a capo, at the fret indicated at the top of the song, to play along.

The pictures below show you all you need to know!

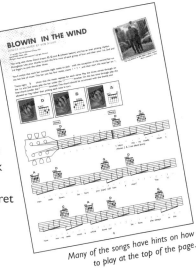

*Many of the songs have hints on how to play at the top of the page.*

## CHORD BOXES

*Chord box for a **D** chord.*

Chord boxes are diagrams of the guitar neck viewed head upwards, face on. They show where to place your fingers to play each chord. Each time you see a new chord box, change to the new chord.

The top line is the nut, the others are the frets. The vertical lines are the strings, starting from E (or 6th) on the left to E (or 1st) on the right.

The black dots indicate where to place your fingers. Strings marked with an O are played open, not fretted; strings marked with an X should not be played. You won't always pick every note of every chord shape that you finger, but it is important to hold each chord in full to learn properly.

## FINGERPICKING

At the start of each song, you'll see the guitar headstock and the strings of the guitar, viewed as if you were playing. The crosses on the strings show each note to be picked with your picking hand.

Usually, you'll play the first note of each group of four with your thumb (**T**), and the other notes with your 1st (**1**), 2nd (**2**) and 3rd (**3**) fingers. This is shown above some of the patterns as a guide. Follow these fingerings and you'll be playing all the fingerpicking patterns in this book in no time!

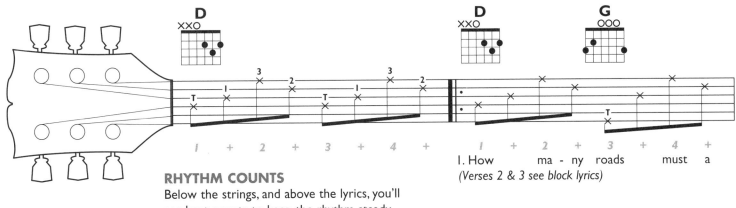

## RHYTHM COUNTS

Below the strings, and above the lyrics, you'll see beat counts to keep the rhythm steady. Each number (or **+**) is a note to pick.

1. How  ma - ny  roads  must  a
*(Verses 2 & 3 see block lyrics)*

# BLOWIN' IN THE WIND
## WORDS AND MUSIC BY BOB DYLAN

This song uses three chord shapes: **D**, **G** and **A** (shown below), and has an even picking rhythm throughout. Use your thumb to pick the first note of each group of four, and then your 1st, 2nd and 3rd fingers to pick the other three.

You'll notice that each bar contains eight notes to pick – with the exception of the second bar on the last line of music. This bar just has four notes; count '*1 + 2 +*', and then start the next bar on '*1*'.

These signs – ||: :|| – show that the music repeats for each verse. Play the three verses through; on the 1st and 2nd times, play the bar under the [1, 2._____] bracket. On the last time through, play the final chord (under the [3._____] bracket). This chord should be strummed with the thumb and allowed to ring rather than picking each note in turn.

This song featured on Bob Dylan's classic second album, released in 1963.

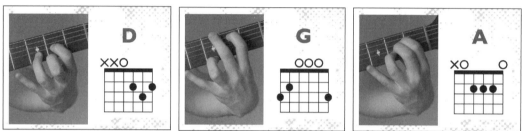

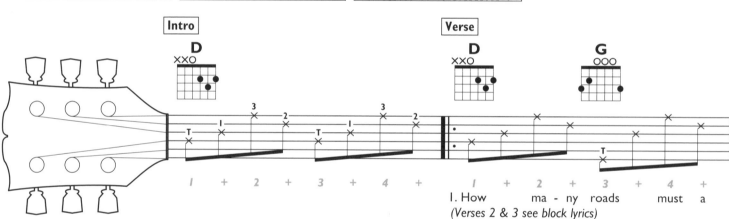

1. How ma - ny roads must a
*(Verses 2 & 3 see block lyrics)*

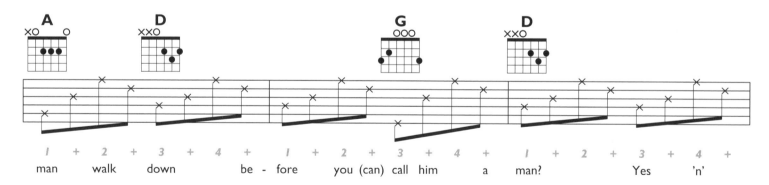

man walk down be - fore you (can) call him a man? Yes 'n'

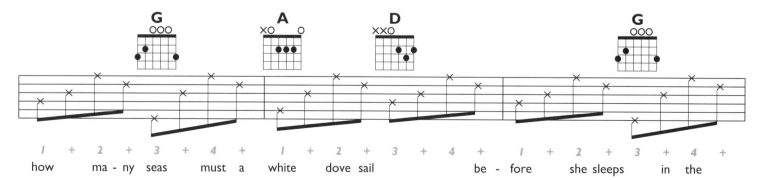

how ma - ny seas must a white dove sail be - fore she sleeps in the

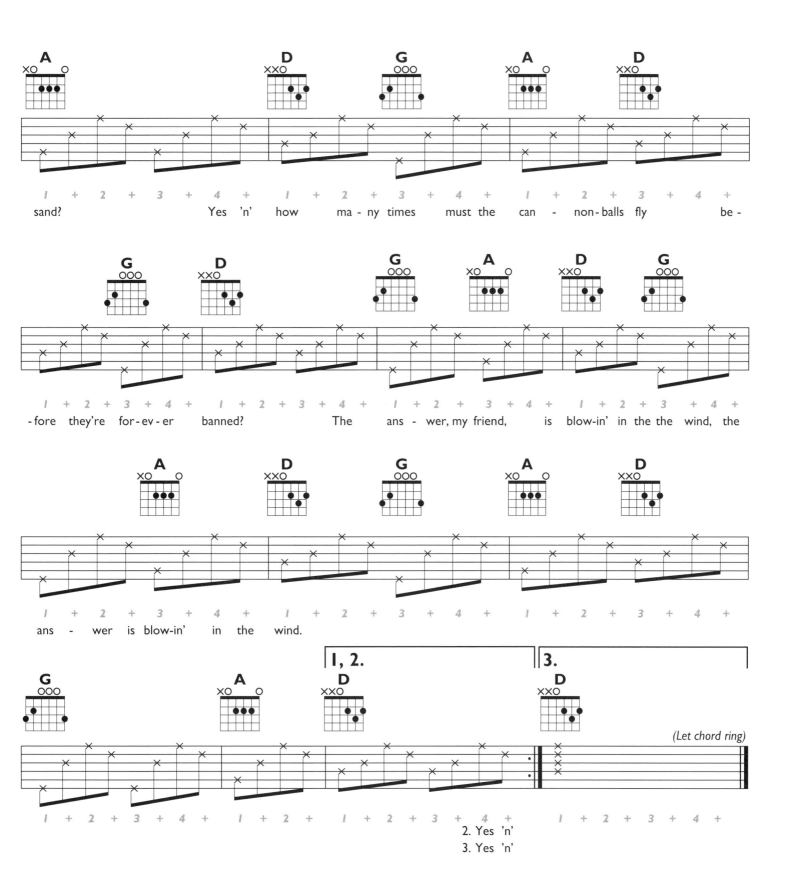

Verse 2:
How many times must a man look up
Before he can see the sky?
Yes, 'n' how many ears must one man have
Before he can hear people cry?
Yes, 'n' how many deaths will it take till he knows
That too many people have died?
The answer, my friend, is blowin' in the wind,
The answer is blowin' in the wind.

Verse 3:
How many years can a mountain exist
Before it's washed to the sea?
Yes, 'n' how many years can some people exist
Before they're allowed to be free?
Yes, 'n' how many times can a man turn his head,
Pretending he just doesn't see?
The answer, my friend, is blowin' in the wind,
The answer is blowin' in the wind.

# MR. TAMBOURINE MAN
## WORDS AND MUSIC BY BOB DYLAN

Some of the picking patterns in this song – for instance, in the first bar – require you to pick two strings at once. Play the first two notes with your thumb and 1st finger, and then the two-note chord with your thumb and 3rd finger, as shown in the photo. The last note of the four is played with your 2nd finger.

The **5° go to ⊕** instruction shows that on the 5th time through the music, jump to the ⊕ section to end the song.

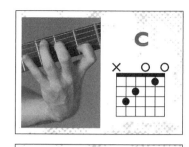

*Picking two notes at once.*

**CAPO: 5TH FRET**

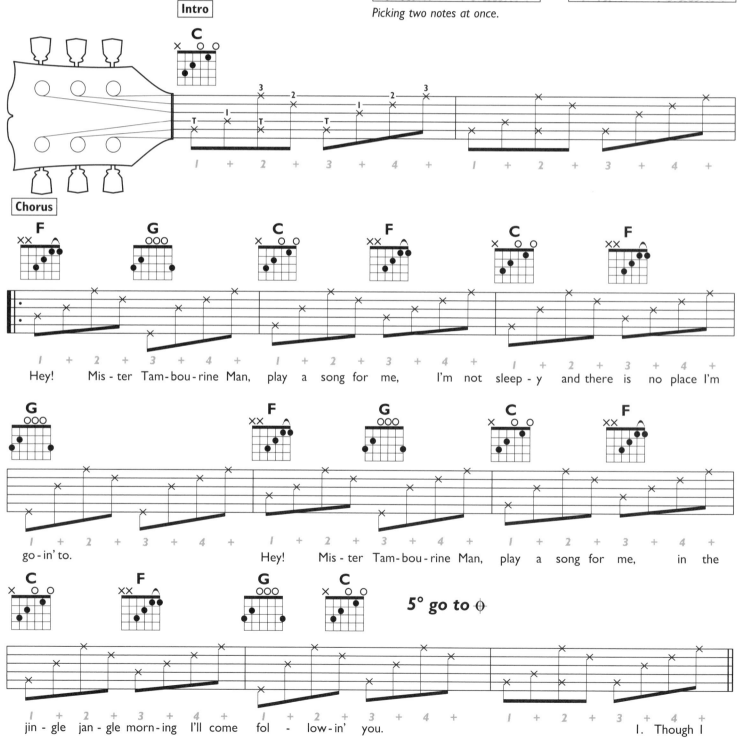

Hey!   Mis - ter   Tam-bou-rine   Man,   play   a   song   for   me,   I'm   not   sleep - y   and   there   is   no   place   I'm

go - in' to.   Hey!   Mis - ter   Tam-bou-rine   Man,   play   a   song   for   me,   in   the

**5° go to ⊕**

jin - gle   jan - gle   morn - ing   I'll   come   fol - low-in'   you.   1. Though I

6

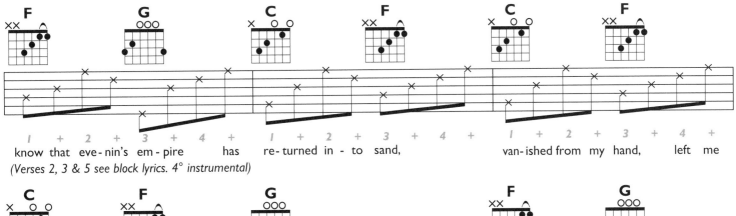
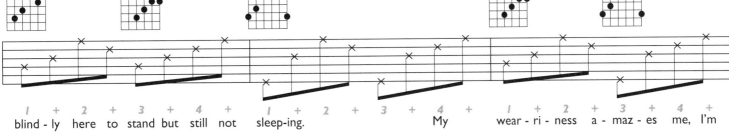

know that eve-nin's em-pire has re-turned in-to sand, van-ished from my hand, left me

*(Verses 2, 3 & 5 see block lyrics. 4° instrumental)*

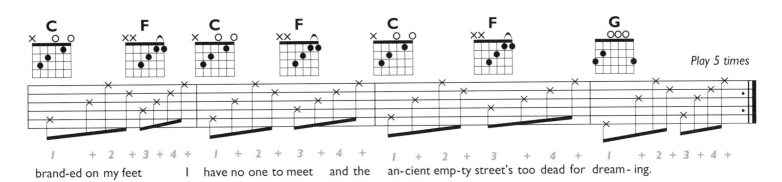

blind-ly here to stand but still not sleep-ing. My wear-ri-ness a-maz-es me, I'm

brand-ed on my feet I have no one to meet and the an-cient emp-ty street's too dead for dream-ing.

*Play 5 times*

*Repeat to fade*

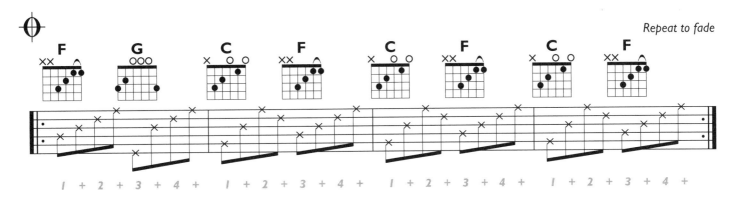

*Verse 2:*
Take me on a trip upon your magic swirlin' ship,
My senses have been stripped, my hands can't feel to grip,
My toes too numb to step, wait only for my boot heels
To be wanderin'.
I'm ready to go anywhere, I'm ready for to fade
Into my own parade, cast your dancing spell my way,
I promise to go under it.

*Verse 3:*
Though you might hear laughin', spinnin', swingin' madly across the sun,
It's not aimed at anyone, it's just escapin' on the run
And but for the sky there are no fences facin'.
And if you hear vague traces of skippin' reels of rhyme
To your tambourine in time, it's just a ragged clown behind,
I wouldn't pay it any mind, it's just a shadow you're
Seein' that he's chasing.

*Verse 5:*
Then take me disappearin' through the smoke rings of my mind,
Down the foggy ruins of time, far past the frozen leaves,
The haunted, frightened trees, out to the windy beach,
Far from the twisted reach of crazy sorrow.
Yes, to dance beneath the diamond sky with one hand waving free,
Silhouetted by the sea, circled by the circus sands,
With all memory and fate driven deep beneath the waves,
Let me forget about today until tomorrow.

# LIKE A ROLLING STONE
## WORDS AND MUSIC BY BOB DYLAN

Pay close attention to which strings are to be picked for each chord shape in this song.
You won't always be picking the lowest-sounding note of the chord shown in the chord
box. When played correctly you'll hear the familiar 'rising' progression in the verses of this
song come out.

Some of the bars in this song use the ⟮ ⁄. ⟯ symbol. This symbol means that the pattern in
the previous bar is to be repeated exactly.

This song first appeared on this 1965
album, Dylan's first purely electric recording.

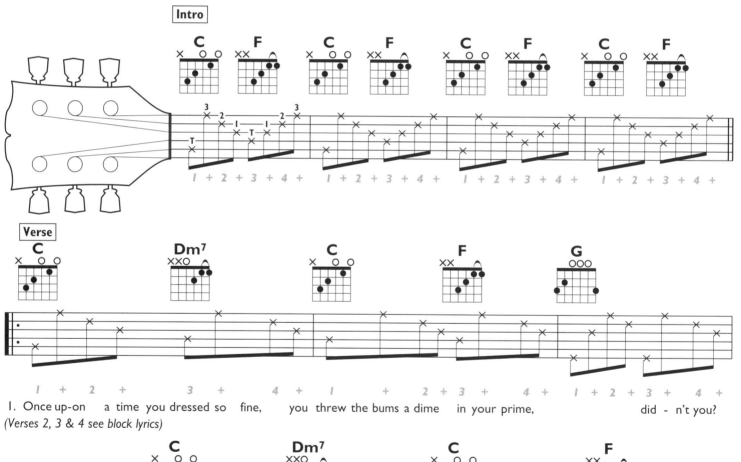

1. Once up-on    a time you dressed so   fine,      you  threw the bums a dime    in your prime,                         did - n't you?
*(Verses 2, 3 & 4 see block lyrics)*

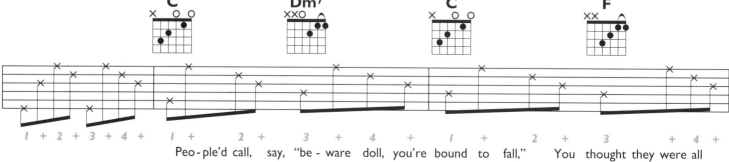

Peo-ple'd call,   say, "be - ware doll, you're bound to  fall,"    You  thought they were all

8

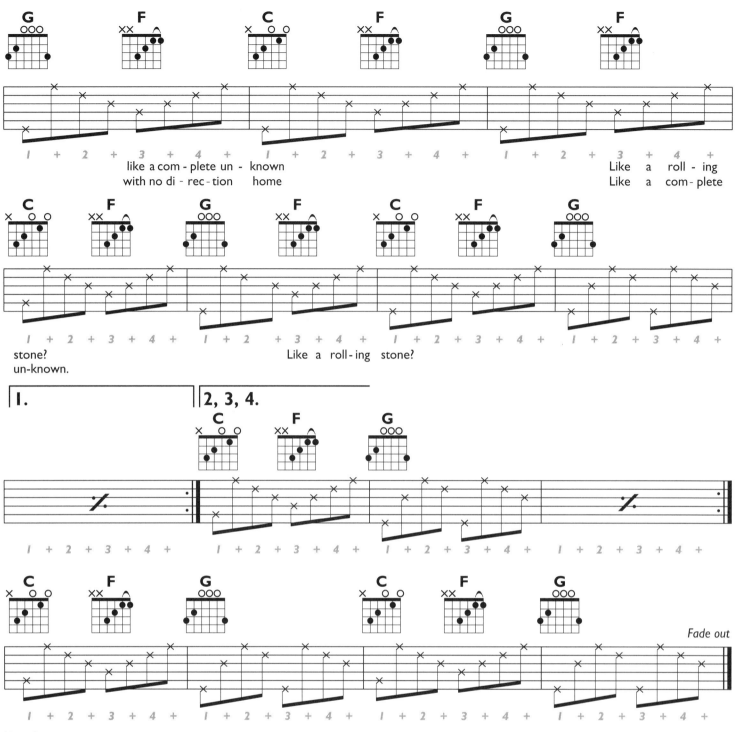

Verse 2:

You've gone to the finest school all right, Miss Lonely
But you know you only used to get juiced in it
And nobody has ever taught you how to live on the street
And now you find out you're gonna have to get used to it
You said you'd never compromise
With the mystery tramp, but now you realize
He's not selling any alibis
As you stare into the vacuum of his eyes
And ask him do you want to make a deal?

Verse 3:

You never turned around to see the frowns on the jugglers and the clowns
When they all come down and did tricks for you
You never understood that it ain't no good
You shouldn't let other people get your kicks for you
You used to ride on the chrome horse with your diplomat
Who carried on his shoulder a Siamese cat
Ain't it hard when you discover that
He really wasn't where it's at
After he took from you everything he could steal.

Verse 4:

Princess on the steeple and all the pretty people
They're drinkin', thinkin' that they got it made
Exchanging all kinds of precious gifts and things
But you'd better lift your diamond ring, you'd better pawn it babe
You used to be so amused
At Napoleon in rags and the language that he used
Go to him now, he calls you, you can't refuse
When you got nothing, you got nothing to lose
You're invisible now, you got no secrets to conceal.

# THINGS HAVE CHANGED
## WORDS AND MUSIC BY BOB DYLAN

This song uses four chords – **Em**, **Am**, **B⁷** and **C** – and has a slightly more complicated picking pattern than the previous three songs, where two strings are picked on the first two counts of each group of four. Pick these with your thumb and 2nd finger, and then your thumb and 3rd finger, as shown in the photos on the right.

This same pattern then applies to each chord change (with your thumb on the 5th string for the **Am**, **B⁷** and **C** chords). Start slowly and practice until you can pick these patterns cleanly.

Don't forget: you'll need a capo for this song to play along with the original recording!

*Picking the two-note chords in each bar.*

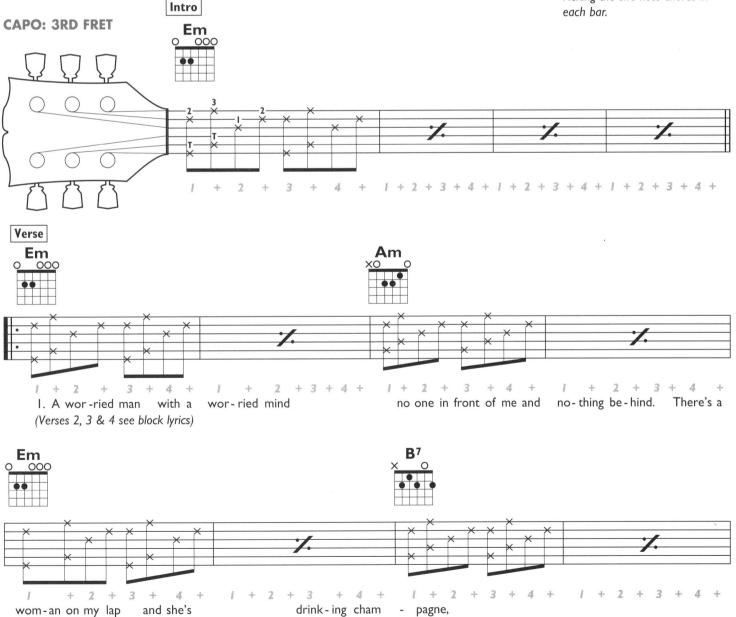

I. A wor-ried man    with a    wor-ried mind            no one in front of me and    no-thing be-hind.    There's a
*(Verses 2, 3 & 4 see block lyrics)*

wom-an on my lap    and she's            drink-ing cham   -   pagne,

11

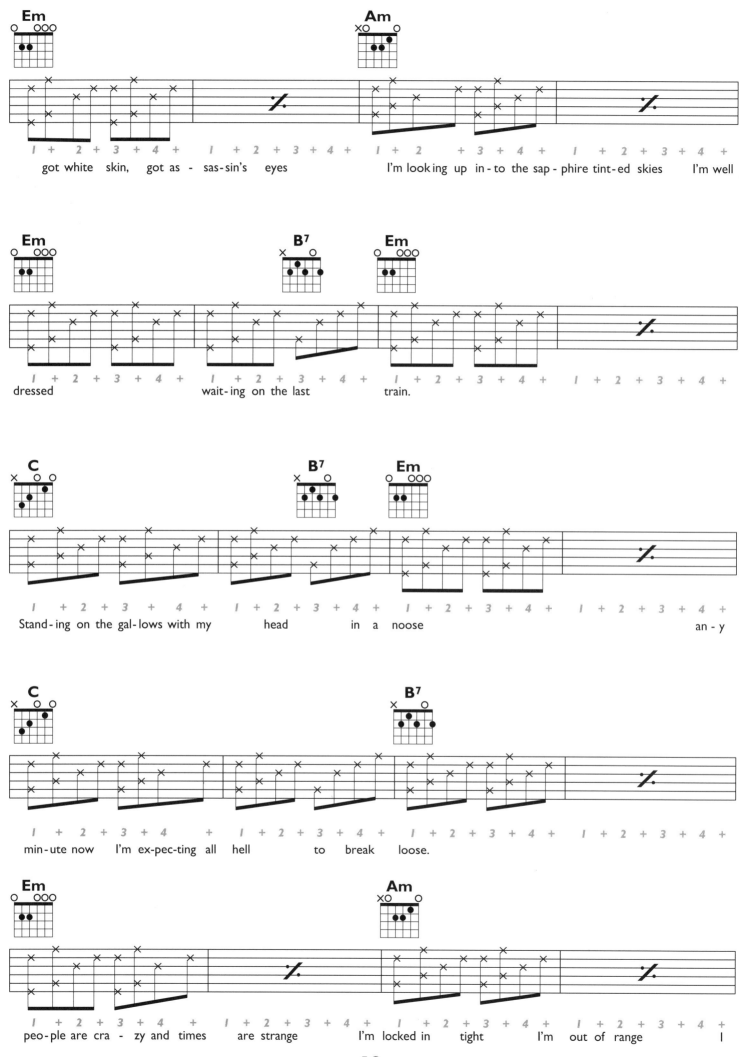

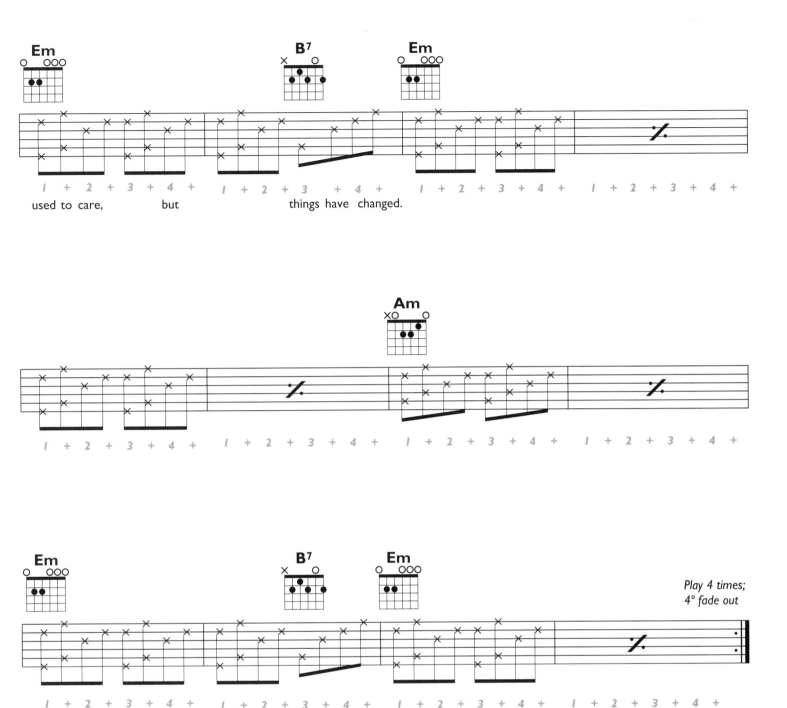

used to care,    but    things have changed.

**Verse 2:**
This place ain't doing me any good
I'm in the wrong town, I should be in Hollywood
Just for a second there I thought I saw something move
Gonna take dancing lessons do the jitterbug rag
Ain't no shortcuts, gonna dress in drag
Only a fool in here would think he's got anything to prove
Lot of water under the bridge, Lot of other stuff too
Don't get up gentlemen, I'm only passing through

**Verse 3:**
I've been walking forty miles of bad road
If the bible is right, the world will explode
I've been trying to get as far away from myself as I can
Some things are too hot to touch
The human mind can only stand so much
You can't win with a losing hand
Feel like falling in love with the first woman I meet
Putting her in a wheel barrow and wheeling her down the street

**Verse 4:**
I hurt easy, I just don't show it
You can hurt someone and not even know it
The next sixty seconds could be like an eternity
Gonna get low down, gonna fly high
All the truth in the world adds up to one big lie
I'm in love with a woman who don't even appeal to me
Mr. Jinx and Miss Lucy, they jumped in the lake
I'm not that eager to make a mistake

# ALL ALONG THE WATCHTOWER
## WORDS AND MUSIC BY BOB DYLAN

This song uses the same four-chord sequence all the way through, and the same fingerpicking pattern throughout. These four chords are: **Am**, **Am/G**, **F**, and **G**. This time, the **F** chord is a full 'barre' shape, as shown in the photo. The curved line in the chord box shows that you 'barre' the strings with your 1st finger. **Am/G** means that you finger a standard **Am** chord shape, but play a different note under the chord with your little finger. In this chord progression the **Am/G** shape creates a smooth bass line between **Am** and **F**.

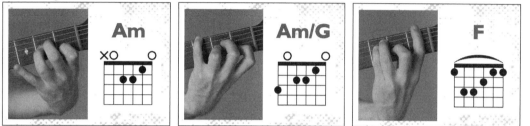

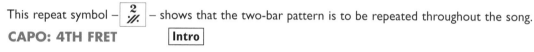

The picking pattern is different for this song. Up till now, the songs have patterns where you only pick the three highest strings with your fingers. In this song, for all chords (except **G**), pick the 2nd, 3rd and 4th strings with your 1st, 2nd and 3rd fingers.

This repeat symbol – 𝄎 – shows that the two-bar pattern is to be repeated throughout the song.

**CAPO: 4TH FRET**

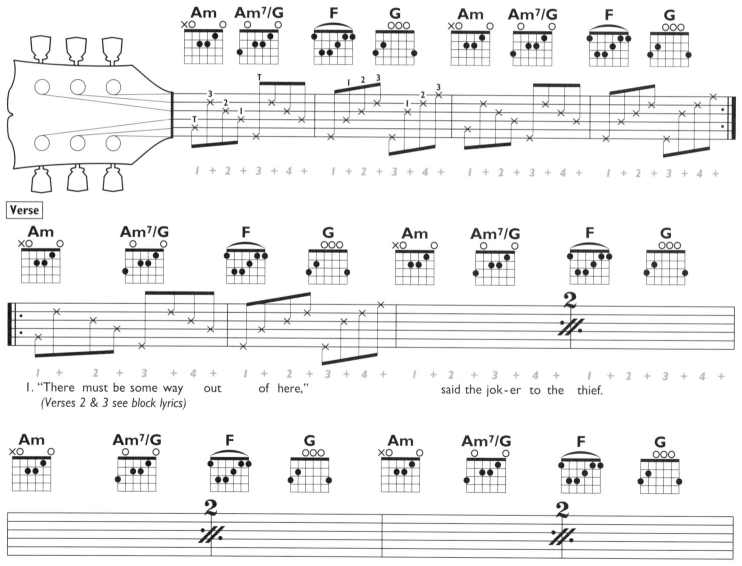

1. "There must be some way      out      of here,"      said the jok-er to the   thief.
   *(Verses 2 & 3 see block lyrics)*

"There's too much   con - fu - sion,      I can't get no re - lief.

14

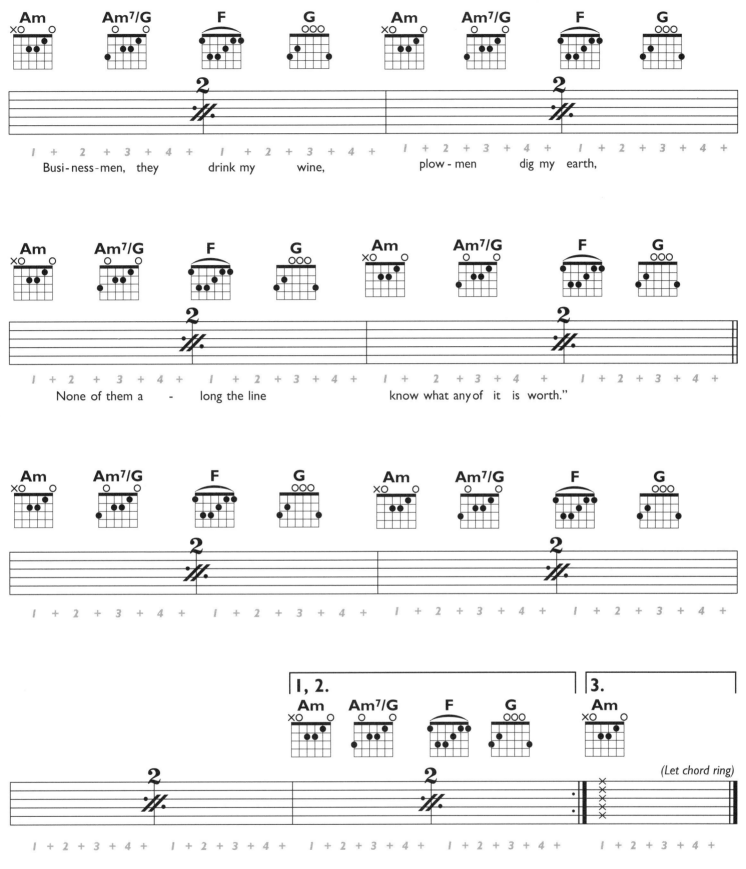

*Verse 2:*
"No reason to get excited," the thief, he kindly spoke,
"There are many here among us who feel that life is but a joke.
But you and I, we've been through that, and this is not our fate,
So let us not talk falsely now, the hour is getting late."

*Verse 3:*
All along the watchtower, princes kept the view
While all the women came and went, barefoot servants, too.
Outside in the distance a wildcat did growl,
Two riders were approaching, the wind began to howl.

# BLIND WILLIE McTELL
## WORDS AND MUSIC BY BOB DYLAN

The **B**♭ chord in this song is a 'barre' shape using the middle four strings of the guitar; barre with your little finger or 3rd finger, as shown in the photo below.

This song uses a longer, eight-note picking pattern for some of the **Dm** chords. Let the first, thumbed note ring out underneath. The **B**♭, **A**⁷ and **C** chords are picked on the middle four strings of the guitar as shown.

This song has a ⊕ section. At the end of the instrumental section, go back to where you see the 𝄋 symbol (at the start of the verse) and then follow the **Go to** ⊕ instruction to jump to the end of the song.

*Blues legend Blind Willie McTell (1901–1959).*

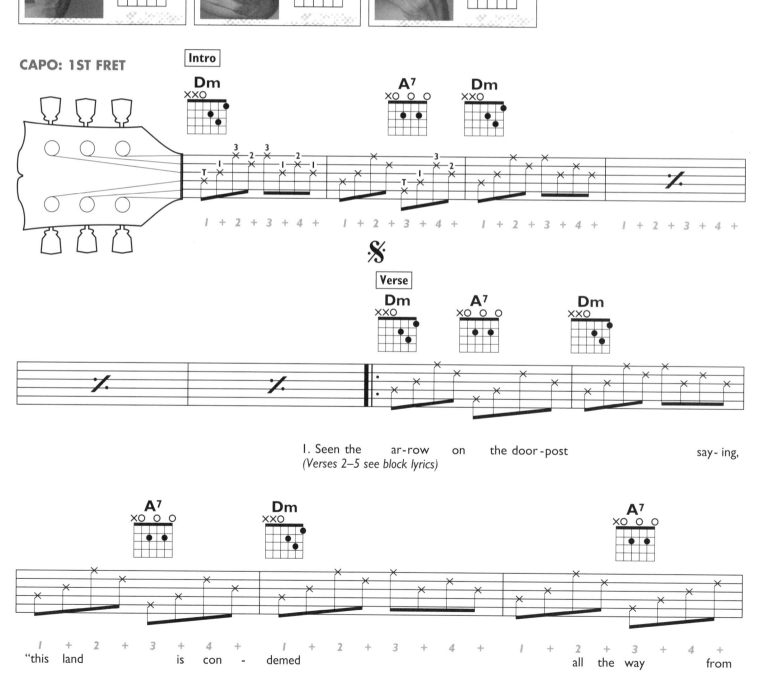

**CAPO: 1ST FRET**

1. Seen the ar-row on the door-post say-ing,
*(Verses 2–5 see block lyrics)*

"this land is con-demed all the way from

16

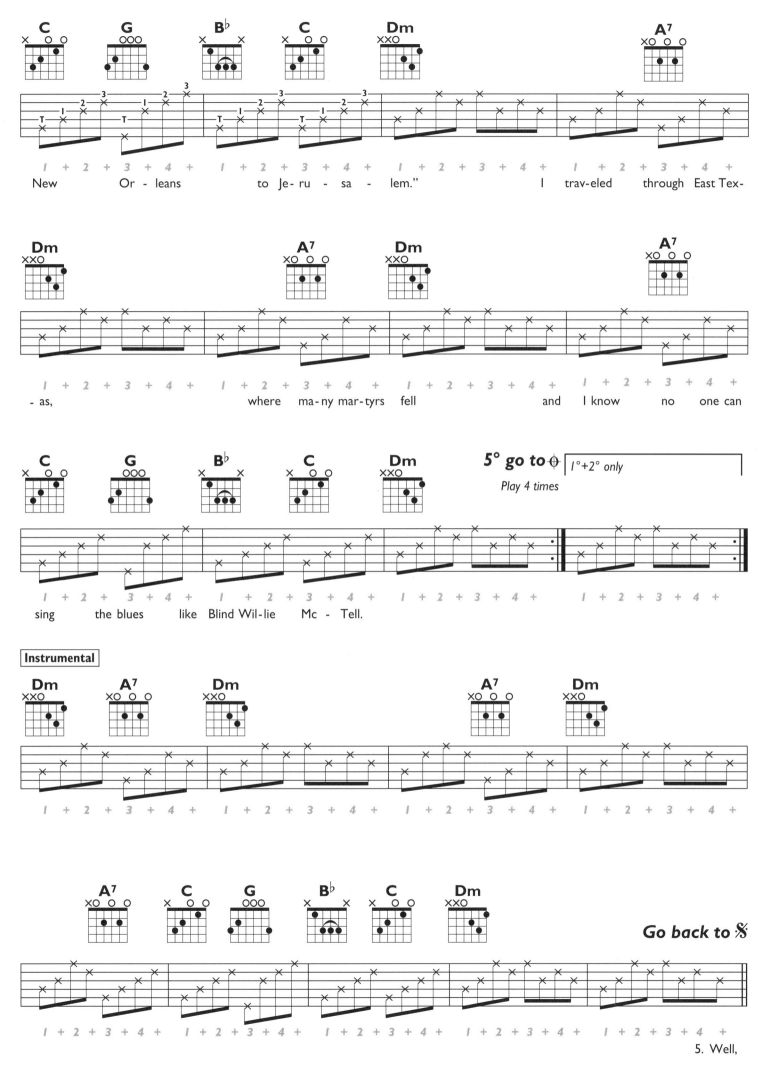

New Or - leans to Je - ru - sa - lem." I trav-eled through East Tex-

- as, where ma-ny mar-tyrs fell and I know no one can

**5° go to ⊕** | *1°+2° only*

*Play 4 times*

sing the blues like Blind Wil-lie Mc - Tell.

**Instrumental**

**Go back to 𝄋**

5. Well,

17

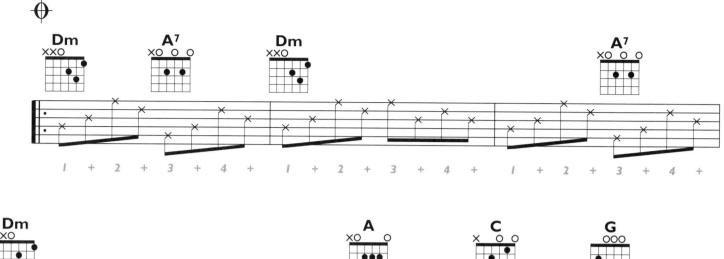

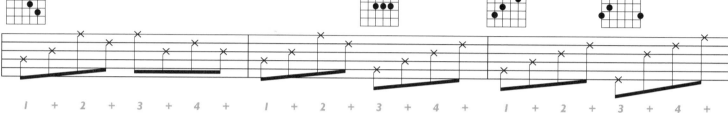

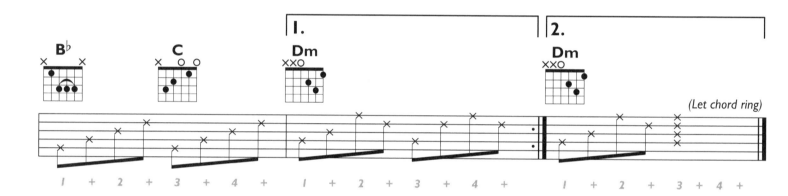

*Verse 2:*

Well, I heard the hoot owl singing
As they were taking down the tents
The stars above the barren trees
Were his only audience
Them charcoal gypsy maidens
Can strut their feathers well
But nobody can sing the blues
Like Blind Willie McTell

*Verse 3:*

See them big plantations burning
Hear the cracking of the whips
Smell that sweet magnolia blooming
(And) see the ghosts of slavery ships
I can hear them tribes a-moaning
(I can) hear the undertaker's bell
(Yeah), nobody can sing the blues
Like Blind Willie McTell

*Verse 4:*

There's a woman by the river
With some fine young handsome man
He's dressed up like a squire
Bootlegged whiskey in his hand
There's a chain gang on the highway
I can hear them rebels yell
And I know no one can sing the blues
Like Blind Willie McTell

*Verse 5:*

Well, God is in His heaven
And we all want what's His
But power and greed and corruptible seed
Seem to be all that there is
I'm gazing out the window
Of the St. James Hotel
And I know no one can sing the blues
Like Blind Willie McTell

# I WANT YOU
## WORDS AND MUSIC BY BOB DYLAN

Dylan's 1966 album Blonde On Blonde.

Like *All Along the Watchtower*, this song features a descending bass line that connects the chord shapes. Pay close attention to the strings to be picked with the right hand so that the smooth progression from **F**, through **Am**, **Dm** to **C** is clear.

Pick the two-note chord at the start of each pattern with your thumb and 3rd finger. For some of the **C** chords, the pattern rises and then falls. Pick the first two notes with your thumb, and you'll be in the right position to pick the other notes.

Look out for the ⊕ and 𝄋 signs in this arrangement.

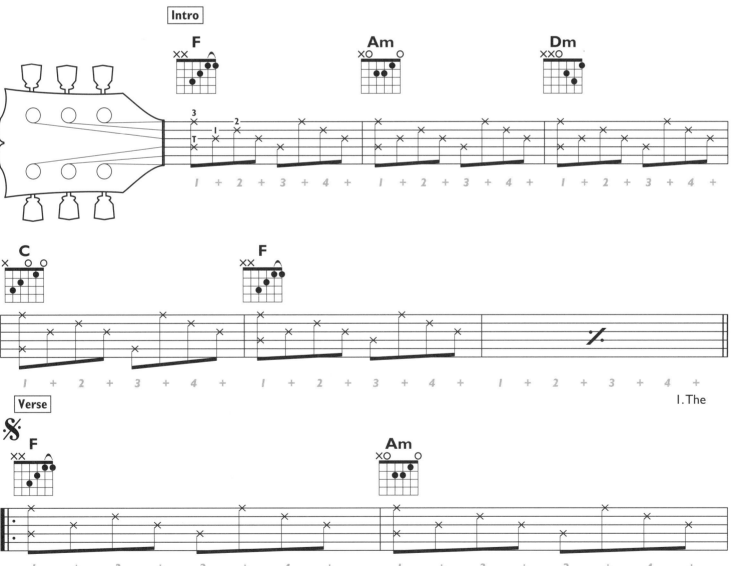

guilt - y un - der - tak - er sighs, the lone - some or - gan grind - er cries, the

*(Veres 2, 3 & 4 see block lyrics)*

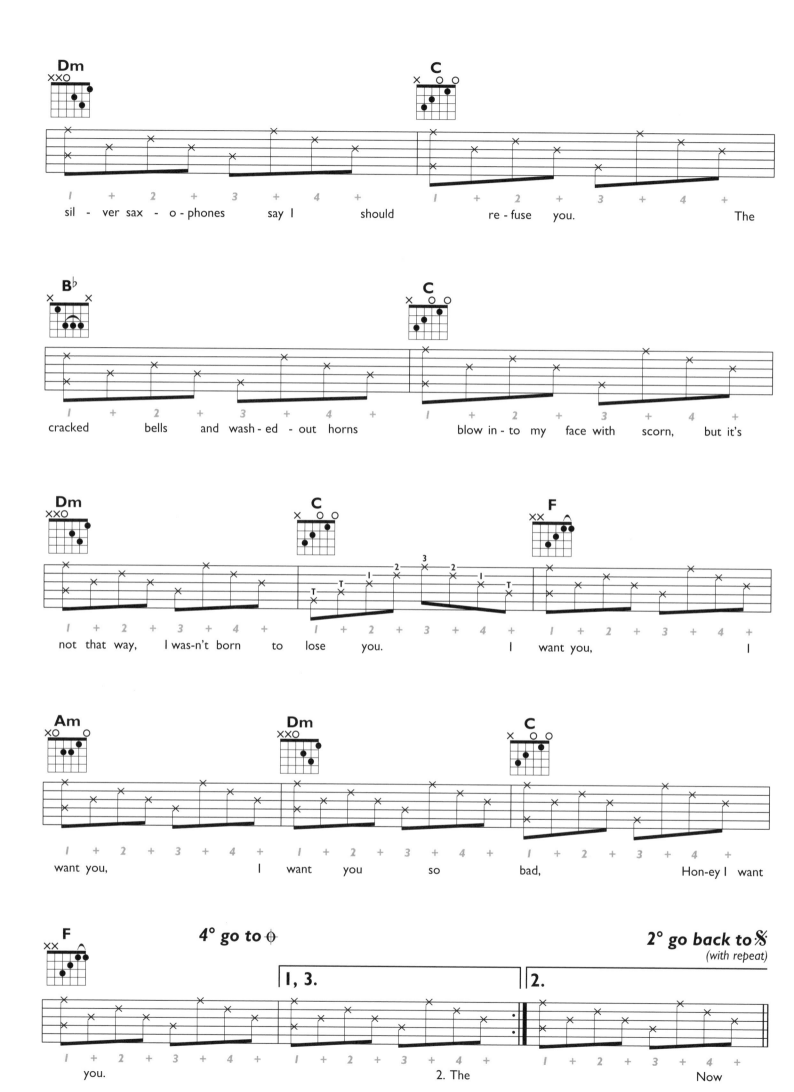

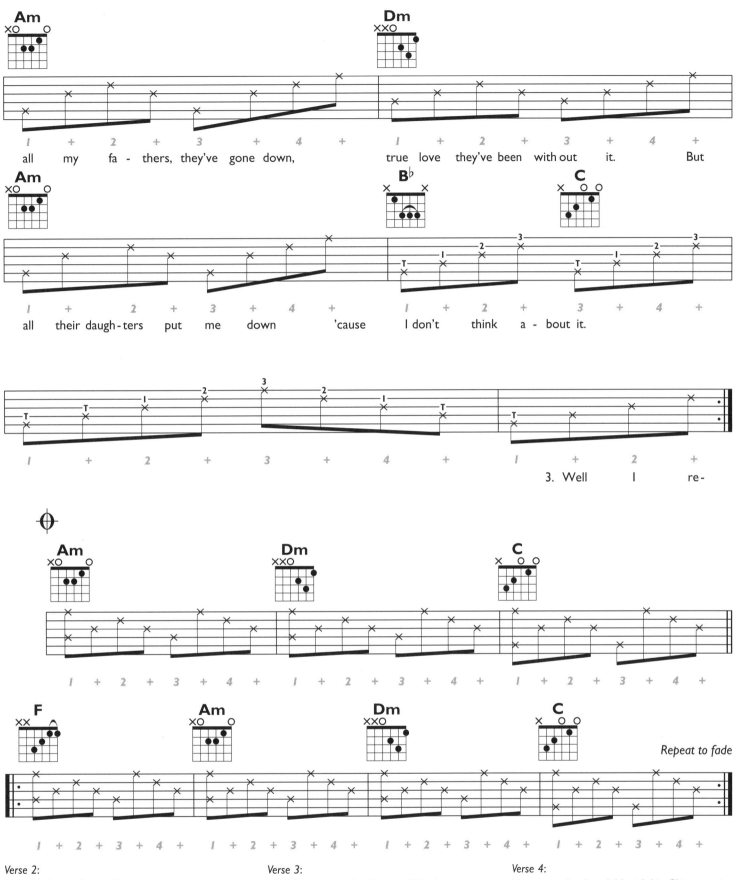

**Verse 2:**

The drunken politician leaps
Upon the street where mothers weep
And the saviors who are fast asleep,
They wait for you.
And I wait for them to interrupt
Me drinkin' from my broken cup
And ask me to
Open up the gate for you.

**Verse 3:**

Well, I return to the Queen of Spades
And talk with my chambermaid.
She knows that I'm not afraid
To look at her.
She is good to me
And there's nothing she doesn't see.
She knows where I'd like to be
But it doesn't matter.

**Verse 4:**

Now your dancing child with his Chinese suit,
He spoke to me, I took his flute.
No, I wasn't very cute to him,
Was I?
But I did it, though, because he lied
Because he took you for a ride
And because time was on his side
And because I . . .

# BOOTS OF SPANISH LEATHER
## WORDS AND MUSIC BY BOB DYLAN

This song uses the following chords: **G**, **C/G**, **Em⁷** and **D/F#**. The **D/F#** chord makes a smooth progression from **Em⁷** to **G**—try playing a normal **D** shape (e.g., on p.4) and hear the difference. The chord shapes are shown in the diagrams below.

Carefully observe the fingering for **G** and **C/G** in these pictures so that you can shift smoothly between these two chords.

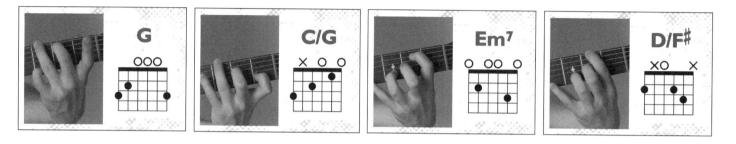

**CAPO: 1ST FRET**

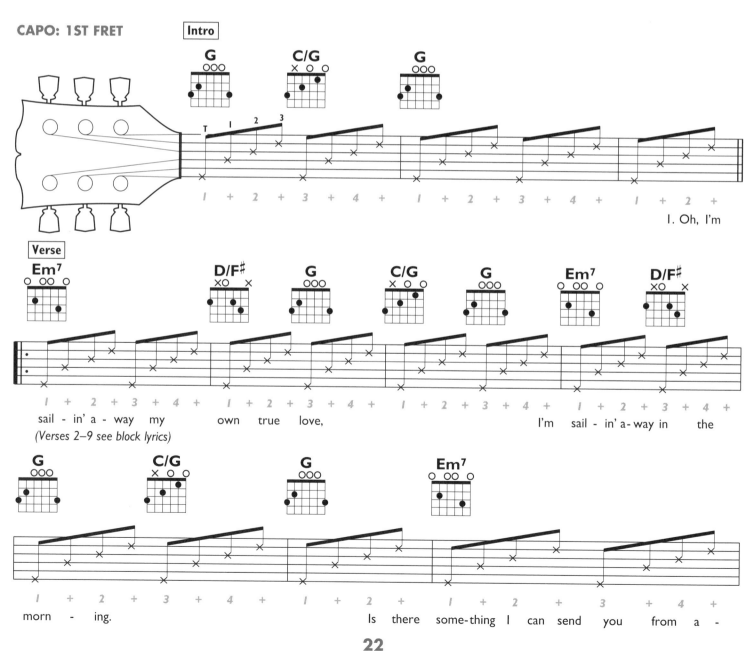

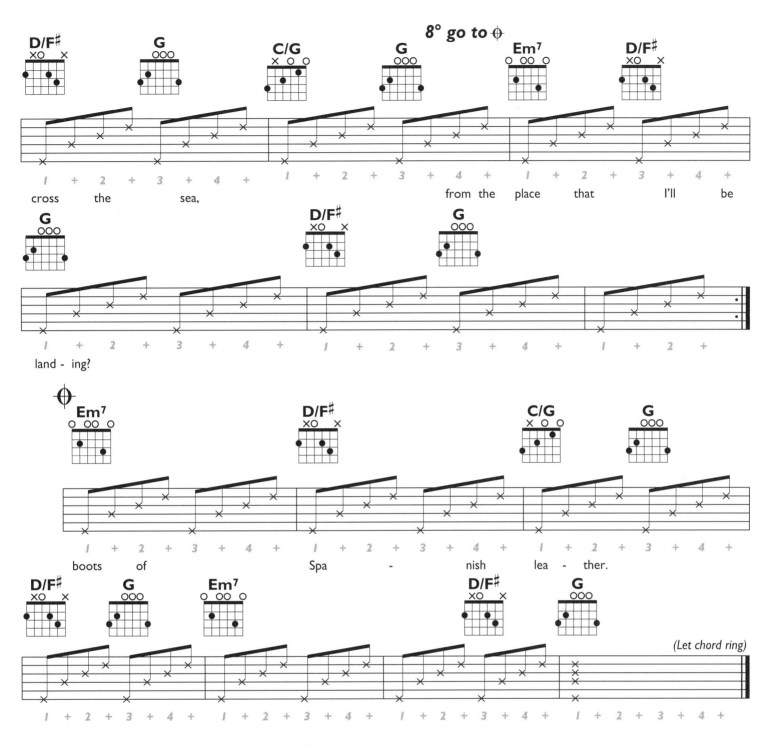

cross the sea, from the place that I'll be land - ing?

boots of Spa - nish lea - ther.

(Let chord ring)

Verse 2:
No, there's nothin' you can send me, my own true love,
There's nothin' I wish to be ownin'.
Just carry yourself back to me unspoiled,
From across that lonesome ocean.

Verse 3:
Oh, but I just thought you might want something fine
Made of silver or of golden,
Either from the mountains of Madrid
Or from the coast of Barcelona.

Verse 4:
Oh, but if I had the stars from the darkest night
And the diamonds from the deepest ocean,
I'd forsake them all for your sweet kiss,
For that's all I'm wishin' to be ownin'.

Verse 5:
That I might be gone a long time
And it's only that I'm askin',
Is there something I can send you to remember me by,
To make your time more easy passin'.

Verse 6:
Oh, how can, how can you ask me again,
It only brings me sorrow.
The same thing I want from you today,
I would want again tomorrow.

Verse 7:
I got a letter on a lonesome day,
It was from her ship a-sailin',
Saying I don't know when I'll be comin' back again,
It depends on how I'm a-feelin'.

Verse 8:
Well, if you, my love, must think that-a-way,
I'm sure your mind is roamin'.
I'm sure your heart is not with me,
But with the country to where you're goin'.

Verse 9:
So take heed, take heed of the western wind,
Take heed of the stormy weather.
And yes, there's something you can send back to me,
Spanish boots of Spanish leather.

# FOREVER YOUNG

## WORDS AND MUSIC BY BOB DYLAN

This song uses the following chords: **D**, **G**, **A**, **A⁷**, **Bm** and **F♯m/C♯**. In the photo you can see how to play the **F♯m/C♯** shape, by 'barring' the top three strings with the first finger.

This song appeared on the 1974 album *Planet Waves*, one of Bob Dylan's numerous collaborations with The Band, led by guitarist Robbie Robertson, pictured above.

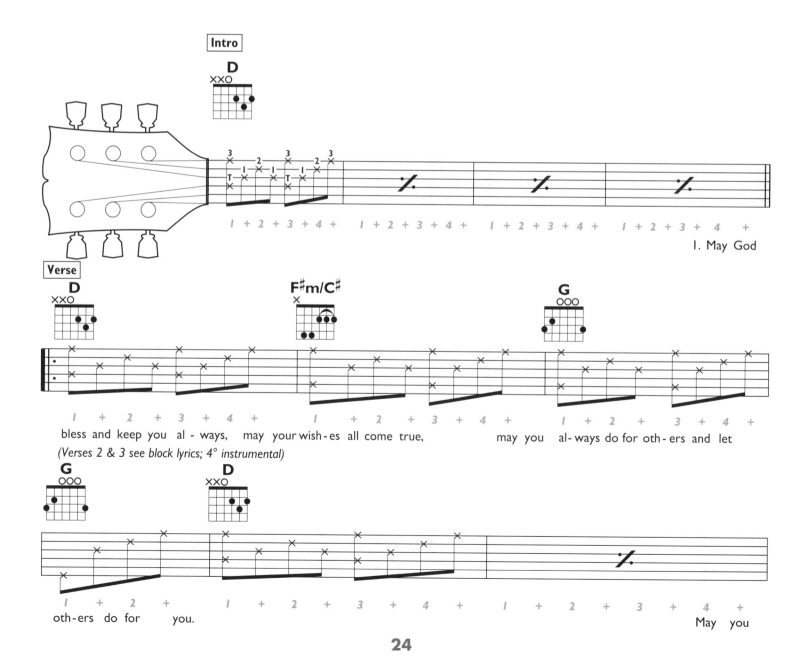

**Intro**

1. May God

**Verse**

bless and keep you al - ways, may your wish - es all come true, may you al - ways do for oth - ers and let

*(Verses 2 & 3 see block lyrics; 4° instrumental)*

oth - ers do for you.

May you

24

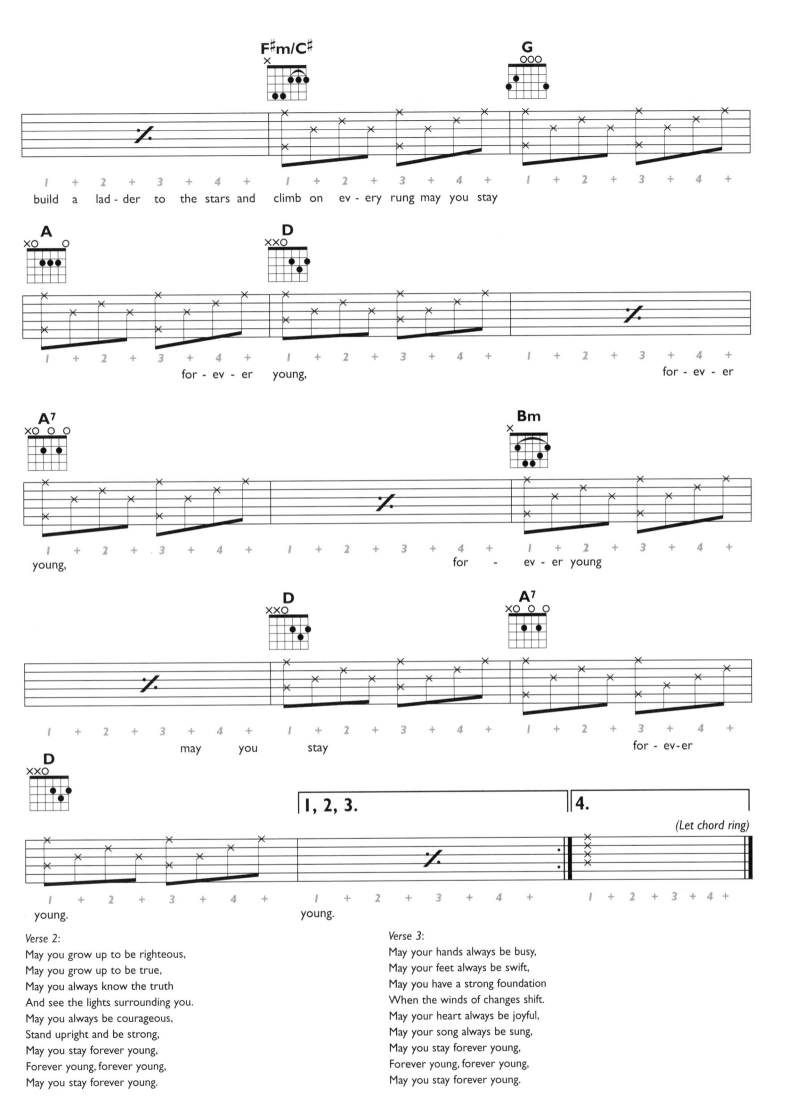

Verse 2:
May you grow up to be righteous,
May you grow up to be true,
May you always know the truth
And see the lights surrounding you.
May you always be courageous,
Stand upright and be strong,
May you stay forever young,
Forever young, forever young,
May you stay forever young.

Verse 3:
May your hands always be busy,
May your feet always be swift,
May you have a strong foundation
When the winds of changes shift.
May your heart always be joyful,
May your song always be sung,
May you stay forever young,
Forever young, forever young,
May you stay forever young.

# TANGLED UP IN BLUE
## WORDS AND MUSIC BY BOB DYLAN

This is another long song, with the verse repeating seven times. The chords for this song are: **A**, **Asus⁴**, **G/A**, **E**, **F♯m** and **D**.

Hear how **Asus⁴** and **G/A** create tension around the chord of **A**; **G/A** is the easiest chord in this book; simply pick the four middle open strings!

Look carefully at the picking patterns; this song uses combinations of picking on all of the strings of the guitar.

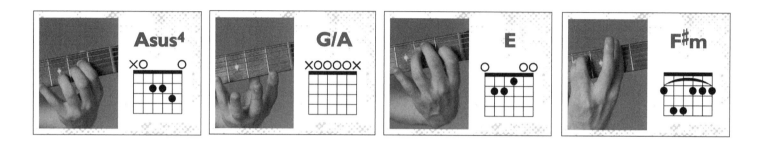

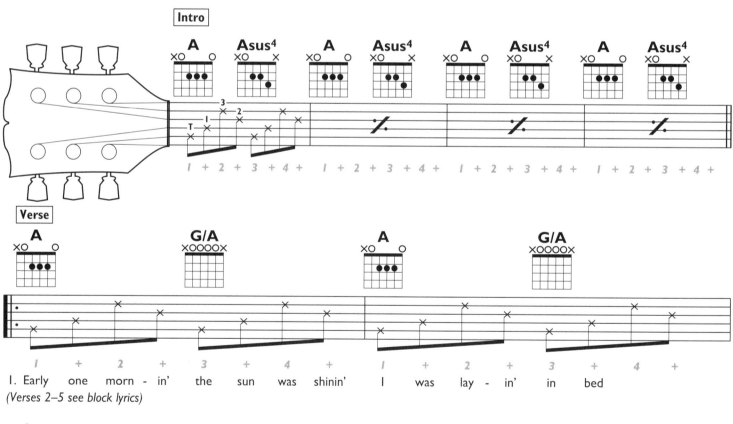

1. Early one morn - in' the sun was shinin' I was lay - in' in bed
*(Verses 2–5 see block lyrics)*

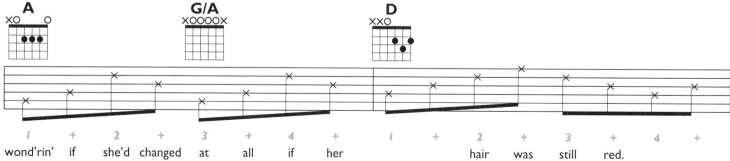

wond'rin' if she'd changed at all if her hair was still red.

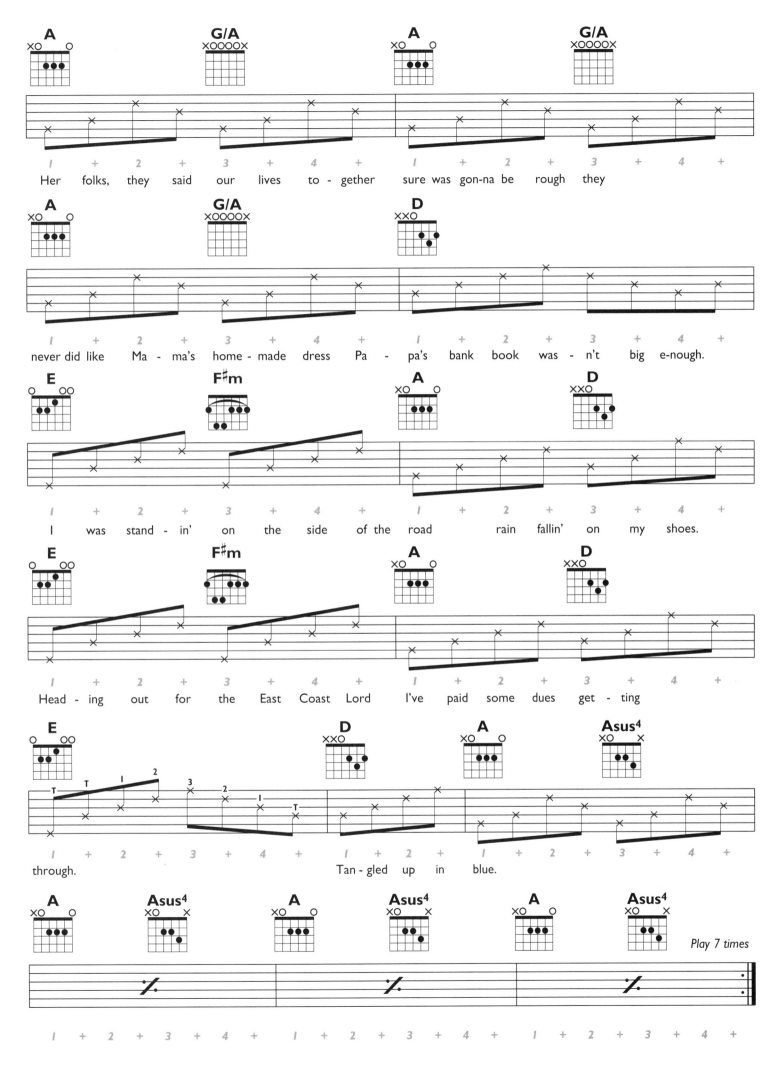

**Instrumental**

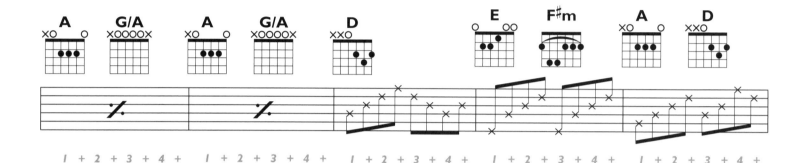

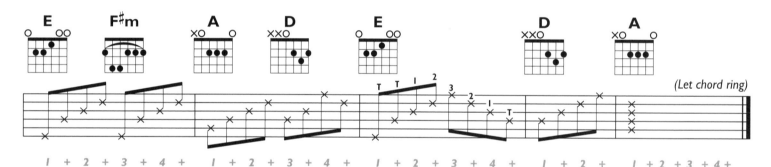

*(Let chord ring)*

*Verse 2:*
She was married when we first met
Soon to be divorced
I helped her out of a jam, I guess,
But I used a little too much force.
We drove that car as far as we could
Abandoned it out West
Split up on a dark sad night
Both agreeing it was best.
She turned around to look at me
As I was walkin' away
I heard her say over my shoulder,
"We'll meet again someday on the avenue,"
Tangled up in blue.

*Verse 3:*
I had a job in the great north woods
Working as a cook for a spell
But I never did like it all that much
And one day the ax just fell.
So I drifted down to New Orleans
Where I happened to be employed
Workin' for a while on a fishin' boat
Right outside of Delacroix.
But all the while I was alone
The past was close behind,
I seen a lot of women
But she never escaped my mind, and I just grew
Tangled up in blue.

*Verse 4:*
She was workin' in a topless place
And I stopped in for a beer,
I just kept lookin' at the side of her face
In the spotlight so clear.
And later on as the crowd thinned out
I's just about to do the same,
She was standing there in back of my chair
Said to me, "Don't I know your name?"
I muttered somethin' underneath my breath,
She studied the lines on my face.
I must admit I felt a little uneasy
When she bent down to tie the laces of my shoe,
Tangled up in blue.

*Verse 5:*
She lit a burner on the stove and offered me a pipe
"I thought you'd never say hello," she said
"You look like the silent type."
Then she opened up a book of poems
And handed it to me
Written by an Italian poet
From the thirteenth century.
And every one of them words rang true
And glowed like burnin' coal
Pourin' off of every page
Like it was written in my soul from me to you,
Tangled up in blue.

*Verse 6:*
I lived with them on Montague Street
In a basement down the stairs,
There was music in the cafes at night
And revolution in the air.
Then he started into dealing with slaves
And something inside of him died.
She had to sell everything she owned
And froze up inside.
And when finally the bottom fell out
I became withdrawn,
The only thing I knew how to do
Was to keep on keepin' on like a bird that flew,
Tangled up in blue.

*Verse 7:*
So now I'm goin' back again,
I got to get to her somehow.
All the people we used to know
They're an illusion to me now.
Some are mathematicians
Some are carpenter's wives.
Don't know how it all got started,
I don't know what they're doin' with their lives.
But me, I'm still on the road
Headin' for another joint
We always did feel the same,
We just saw it from a different point of view,
Tangled up in blue.

28

# YOU'RE GONNA MAKE ME LONESOME WHEN YOU GO

## WORDS AND MUSIC BY BOB DYLAN

The new chords for this song are **G⁷** and **D⁷**. These are similar chord shapes to **G** and **D**.

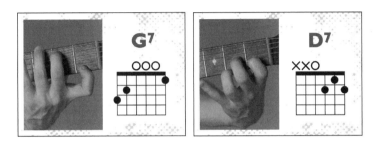

**CAPO: 4TH FRET**

**Intro**

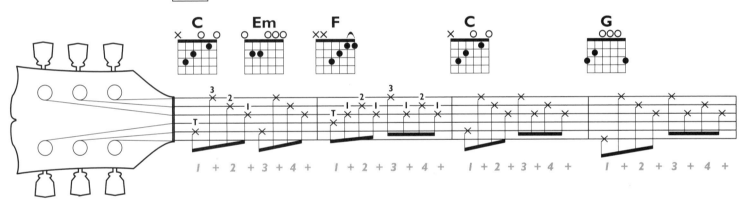

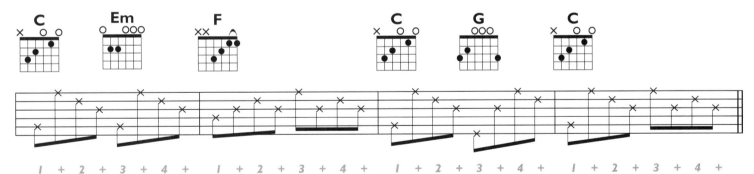

**Verse**

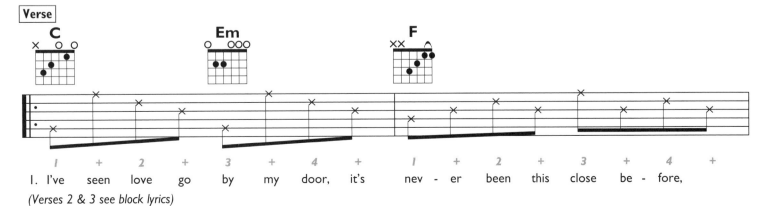

1. I've   seen   love   go   by   my   door,   it's   nev - er   been   this   close   be - fore,

*(Verses 2 & 3 see block lyrics)*

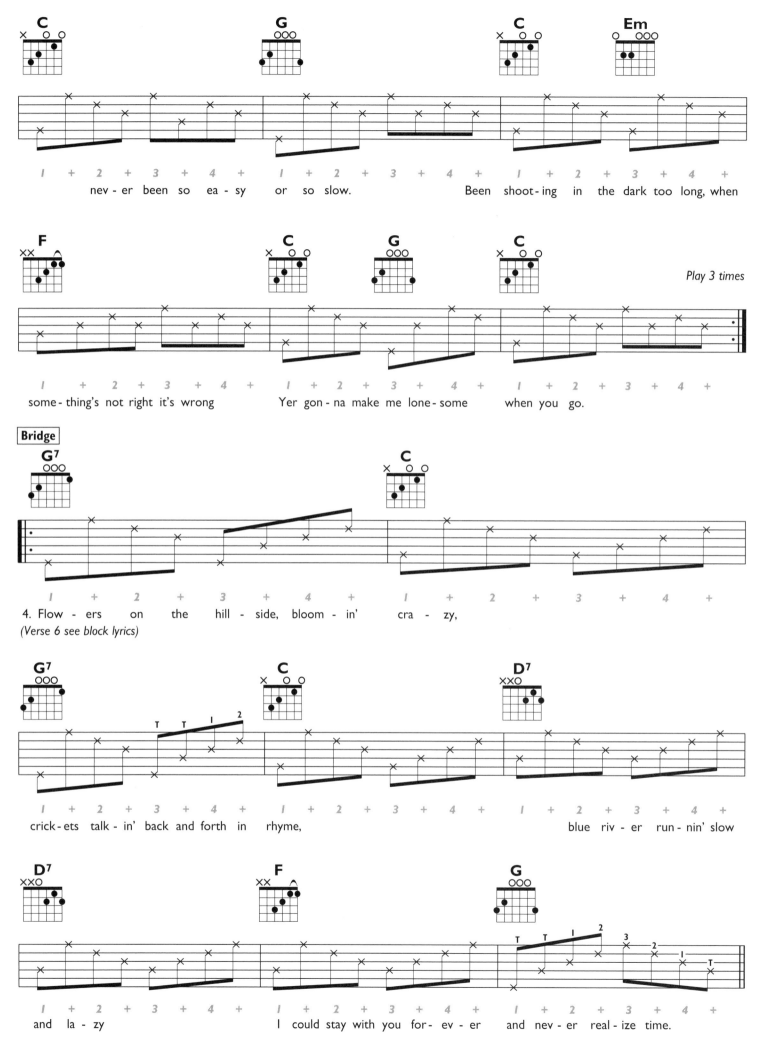

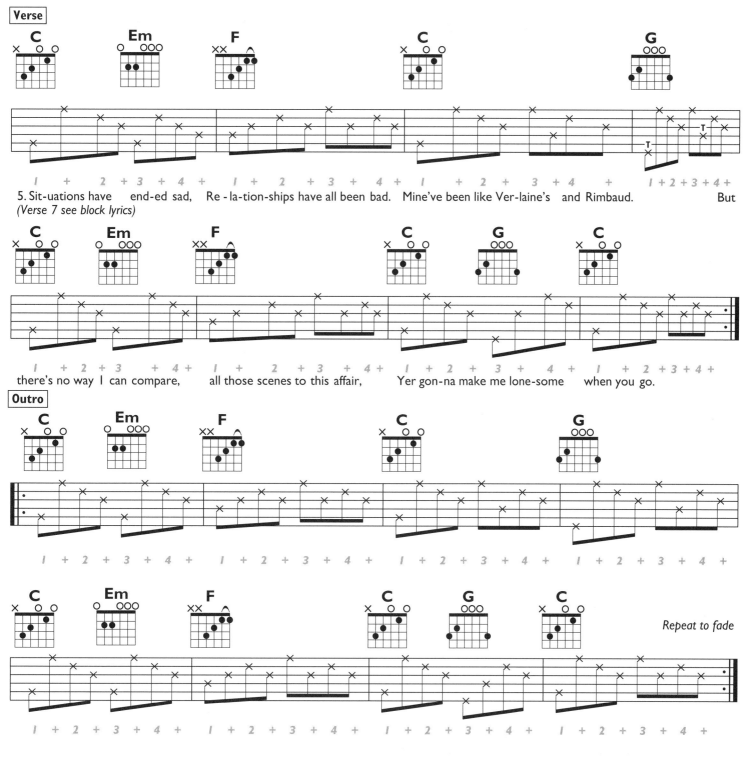

**Verse**

5. Sit-uations have ... end-ed sad, Re - la-tion-ships have all been bad. Mine've been like Ver-laine's ... and Rimbaud. ... But
*(Verse 7 see block lyrics)*

there's no way I can compare, ... all those scenes to this affair, ... Yer gon-na make me lone-some ... when you go.

**Outro**

*Repeat to fade*

---

Verse 2:

Dragon clouds so high above
I've only known careless love,
It's always hit me from below.
This time around it's more correct
Right on target, so direct,
Yer gonna make me lonesome when you go.

Verse 3:

Purple clover, Queen Anne lace,
Crimson hair across your face,
You could make me cry if you don't know.
Can't remember what I was thinkin' of
You might be spoilin' me too much, love,
Yer gonna make me lonesome when you go.

Verse 4:

Flowers on the hillside, bloomin' crazy,
Crickets talkin' back and forth in rhyme,
Blue river runnin' slow and lazy,
I could stay with you forever
And never realize the time.

Verse 5:

Situations have ended sad,
Relationships have all been bad.
Mine've been like Verlaine's and Rimbaud.
But there's no way I can compare
All those scenes to this affair,
Yer gonna make me lonesome when you go.

Verse 6:

Yer gonna make me wonder what I'm doin',
Stayin' far behind without you.
Yer gonna make me wonder what I'm sayin',
Yer gonna make me give myself a good talkin' to.

Verse 7:

I'll look for you in old Honolulu,
San Francisco, Ashtabula,
Yer gonna have to leave me now, I know.
But I'll see you in the sky above,
In the tall grass, in the ones I love,
Yer gonna make me lonesome when you go.

# DON'T THINK TWICE, IT'S ALL RIGHT
**WORDS AND MUSIC BY BOB DYLAN**

This song has the most complex chord progression so far; in the second bar the chords change rather quickly. The chords are: **C**, **G**, **Am**, **Am/G**, **F**, **G⁷**, **C⁷**, **D⁷**, and **C/G**. Look carefully at the picking for **Am** followed by **Am/G**, using your thumb and first finger.

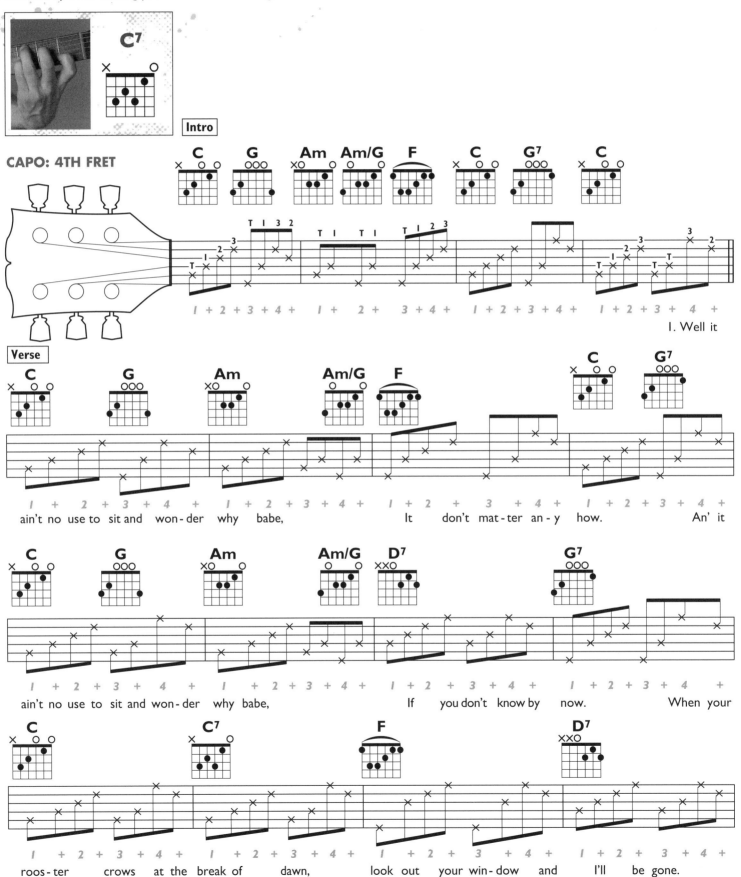

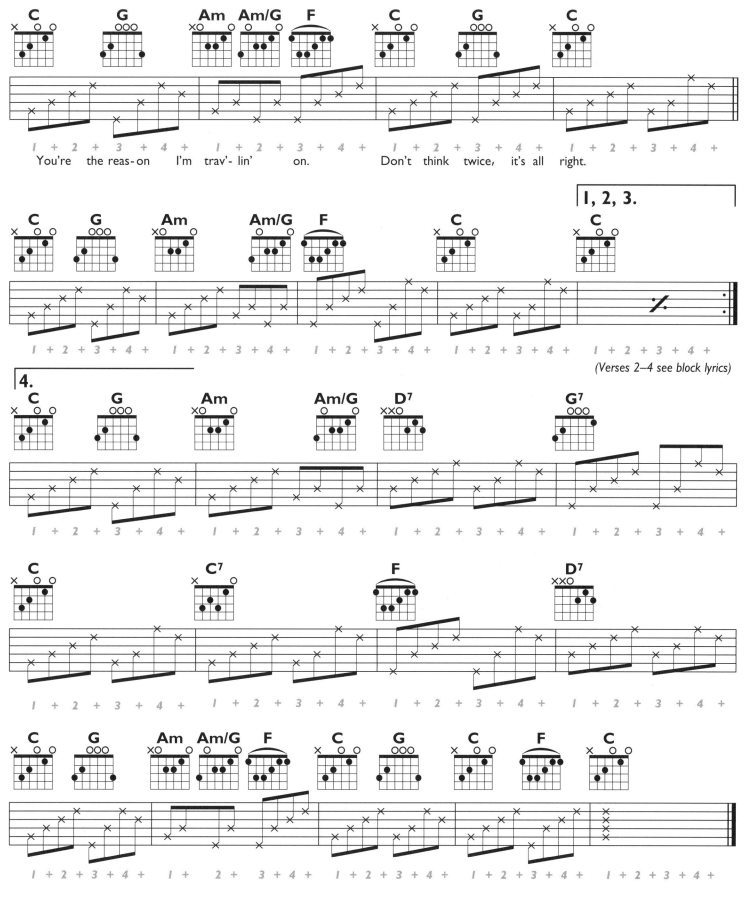

**Verse 2:**
It ain't no use in turnin' on your light, babe
That light I never knowed
An' it ain't no use in turnin' on your light, babe
I'm on the dark side of the road
Still I wish there was somethin' you would do or say
To try and make me change my mind and stay
We never did too much talkin' anyway
So don't think twice, it's all right

**Verse 3:**
It ain't no use in callin' out my name, gal
Like you never did before
It ain't no use in callin' out my name, gal
I can't hear you any more
I'm a-thinkin' and a-wond'rin'
all the way down the road
I once loved a woman, a child I'm told
I give her my heart but she wanted my soul
But don't think twice, it's all right

**Verse 4:**
I'm walkin' down that long, lonesome road, babe
Where I'm bound, I can't tell
But goodbye's too good a word, gal
So I'll just say fare thee well
I ain't sayin' you treated me unkind
You could have done better but I don't mind
You just kinda wasted my precious time
But don't think twice, it's all right

# LAY, LADY, LAY
## WORDS AND MUSIC BY BOB DYLAN

The main chord sequence in this song is **G**, **Bm**, **F** and **Am**.
Pick the two-note chords with your thumb and 3rd finger. The first two notes of the
sequence are both picked with the thumb.

The Nashville skyline… Dylan recorded this song
for his country themed album in 1969.

**CAPO: 2ND FRET**

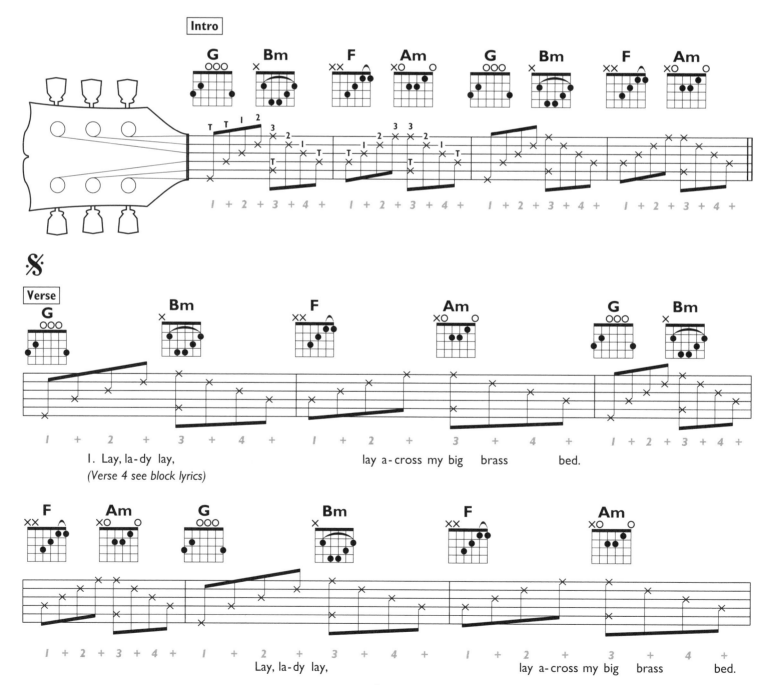

1. Lay, la-dy lay,
(Verse 4 see block lyrics)

lay a-cross my big    brass    bed.

Lay, la-dy lay,

lay a-cross my big    brass    bed.

34

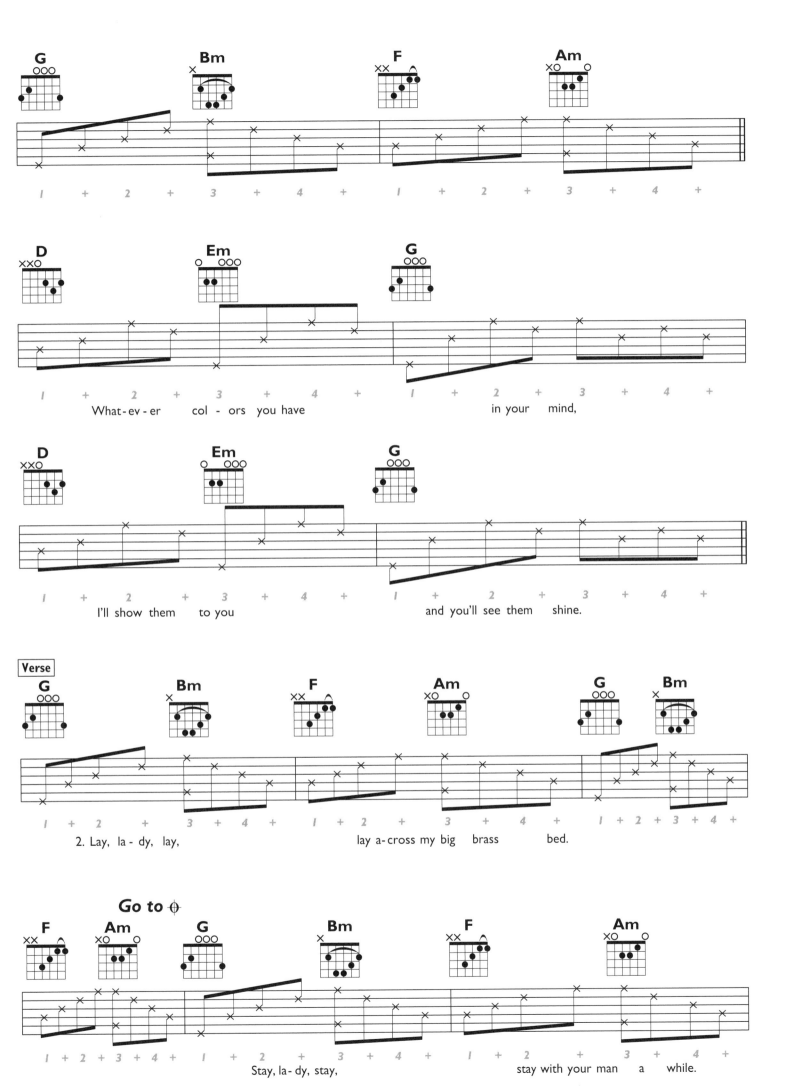

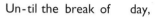

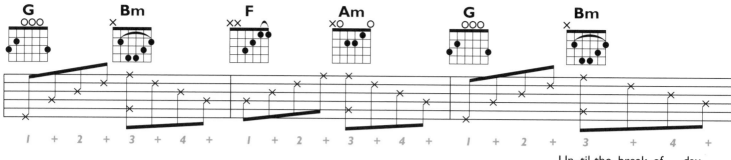

Un-til the break of day,

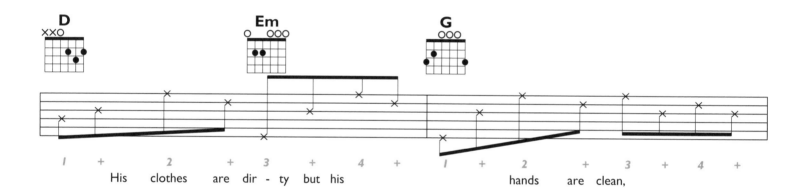

let me see you make him smile.

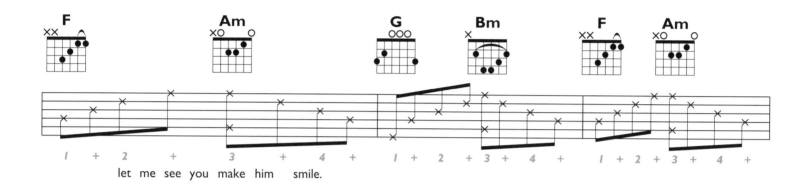

His clothes are dir - ty but his hands are clean,

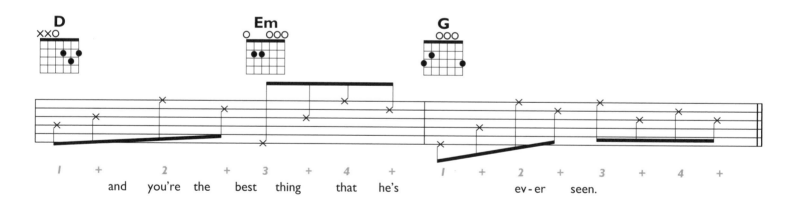

and you're the best thing that he's ev - er seen.

**Verse**

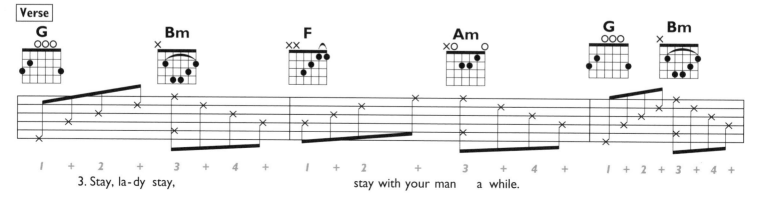

3. Stay, la-dy stay, stay with your man a while.

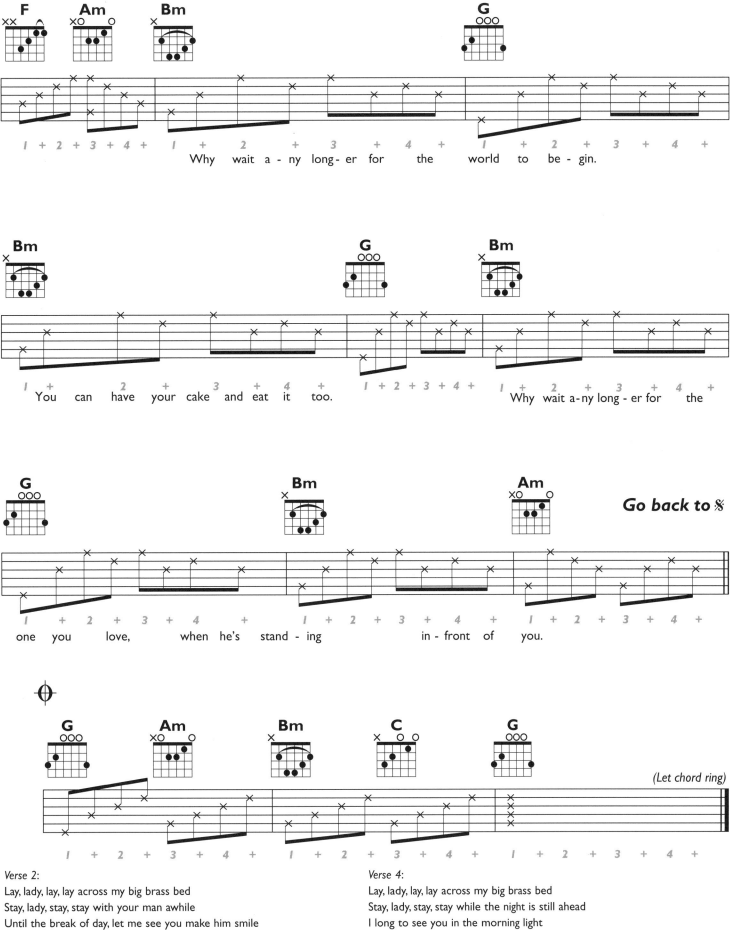

*Verse 2:*
Lay, lady, lay, lay across my big brass bed
Stay, lady, stay, stay with your man awhile
Until the break of day, let me see you make him smile
His clothes are dirty but his hands are clean
And you're the best thing that he's ever seen

*Verse 3:*
Stay, lady, stay, stay with your man awhile
Why wait any longer for the world to begin
You can have your cake and eat it too
Why wait any longer for the one you love
When he's standing in front of you

*Verse 4:*
Lay, lady, lay, lay across my big brass bed
Stay, lady, stay, stay while the night is still ahead
I long to see you in the morning light
I long to reach for you in the night
Stay, lady, stay, stay while the night is still ahead

# MOST OF THE TIME
## WORDS AND MUSIC BY BOB DYLAN

This song was recorded on Bob Dylan's 1989
critically acclaimed album Oh Mercy.

Watch for the quick changes to **G** in this song, and for the bars where the first
two notes of the pattern are played with your thumb.

It might take a little practice to master the **F/G** shape shown below.

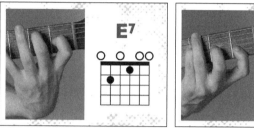

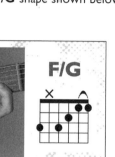

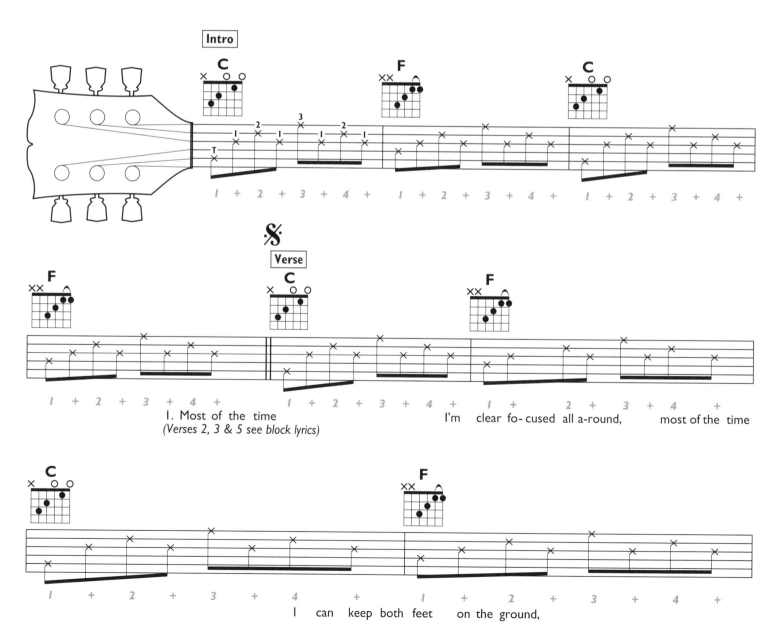

1. Most of the time
*(Verses 2, 3 & 5 see block lyrics)*

I'm clear fo-cused all a-round, most of the time

I can keep both feet on the ground,

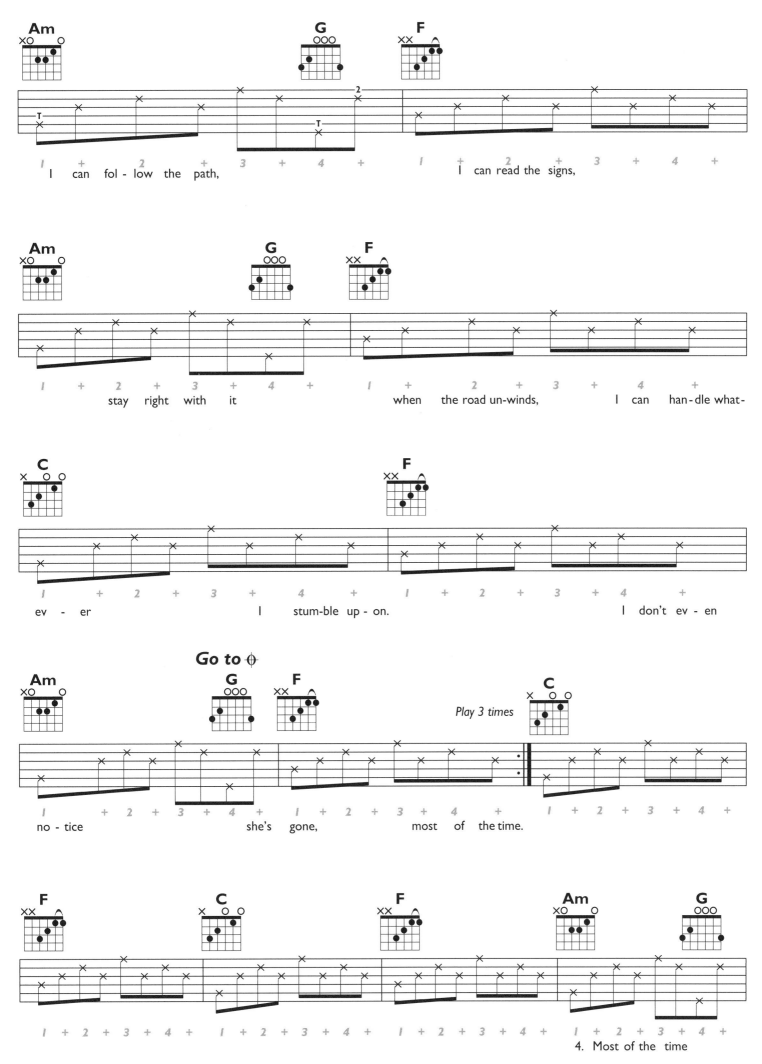

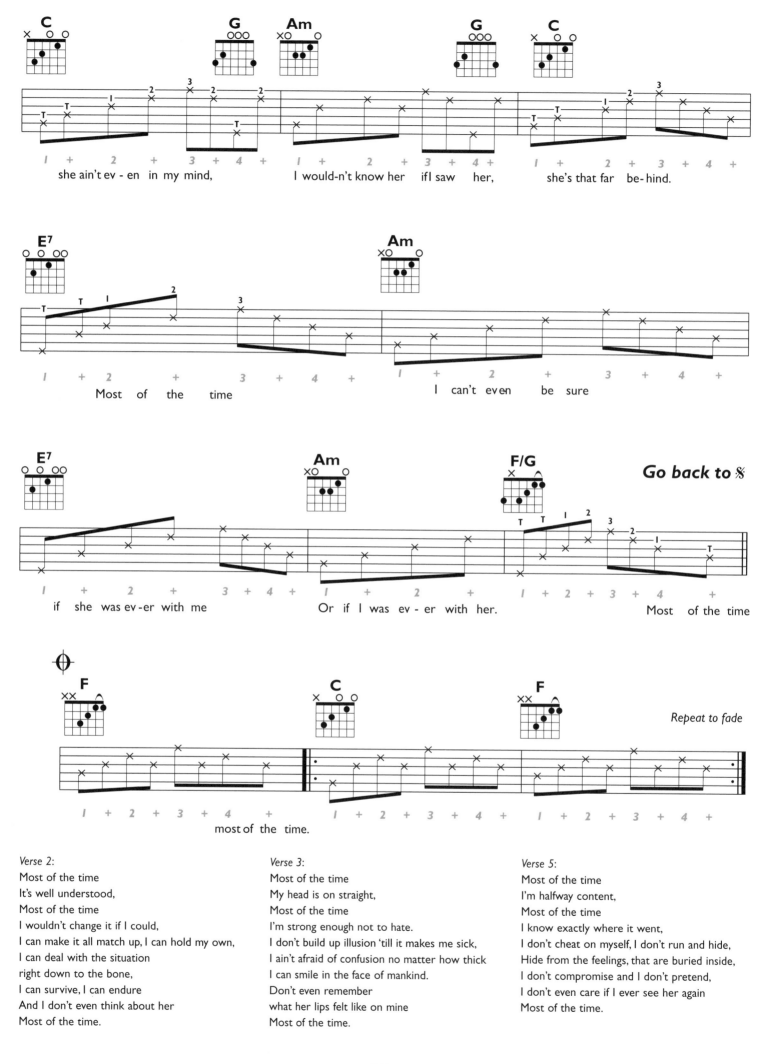

Verse 2:
Most of the time
It's well understood,
Most of the time
I wouldn't change it if I could,
I can make it all match up, I can hold my own,
I can deal with the situation
right down to the bone,
I can survive, I can endure
And I don't even think about her
Most of the time.

Verse 3:
Most of the time
My head is on straight,
Most of the time
I'm strong enough not to hate.
I don't build up illusion 'till it makes me sick,
I ain't afraid of confusion no matter how thick
I can smile in the face of mankind.
Don't even remember
what her lips felt like on mine
Most of the time.

Verse 5:
Most of the time
I'm halfway content,
Most of the time
I know exactly where it went,
I don't cheat on myself, I don't run and hide,
Hide from the feelings, that are buried inside,
I don't compromise and I don't pretend,
I don't even care if I ever see her again
Most of the time.

# NOT DARK YET
## WORDS AND MUSIC BY BOB DYLAN

Pick the two-note chords at the beginning of each pattern as shown in the photos below: thumb & 3rd finger, and then thumb & 2nd finger.

Note the difference between **G/F** and **F/G** from the previous song!

Look at the beat counts carefully; some of the bars have two extra counts.

This song featured on the soundtrack of The Wonder Boys (2000), starring Michael Douglas and Tobey Maguire, above, alongside 'Things Have Changed' (p.11), which won the Academy Award for best original song.

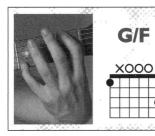

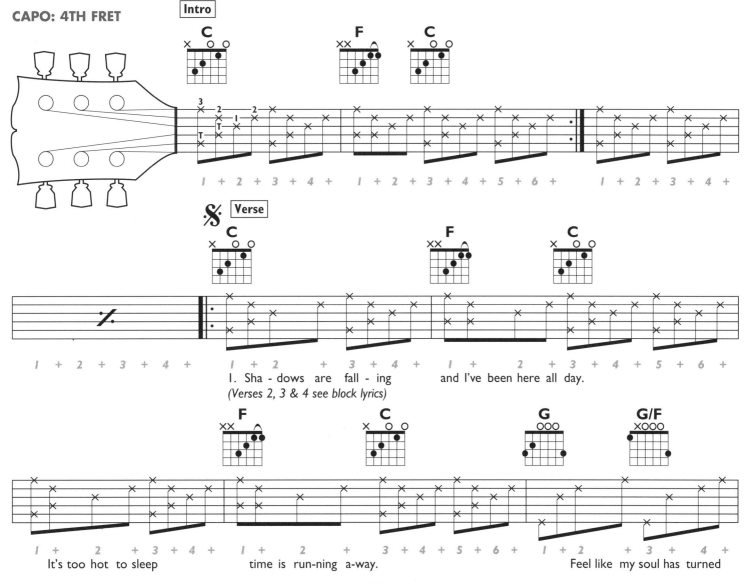

**CAPO: 4TH FRET**

1. Sha - dows are fall - ing and I've been here all day.
*(Verses 2, 3 & 4 see block lyrics)*

It's too hot to sleep time is run-ning a-way. Feel like my soul has turned

**41**

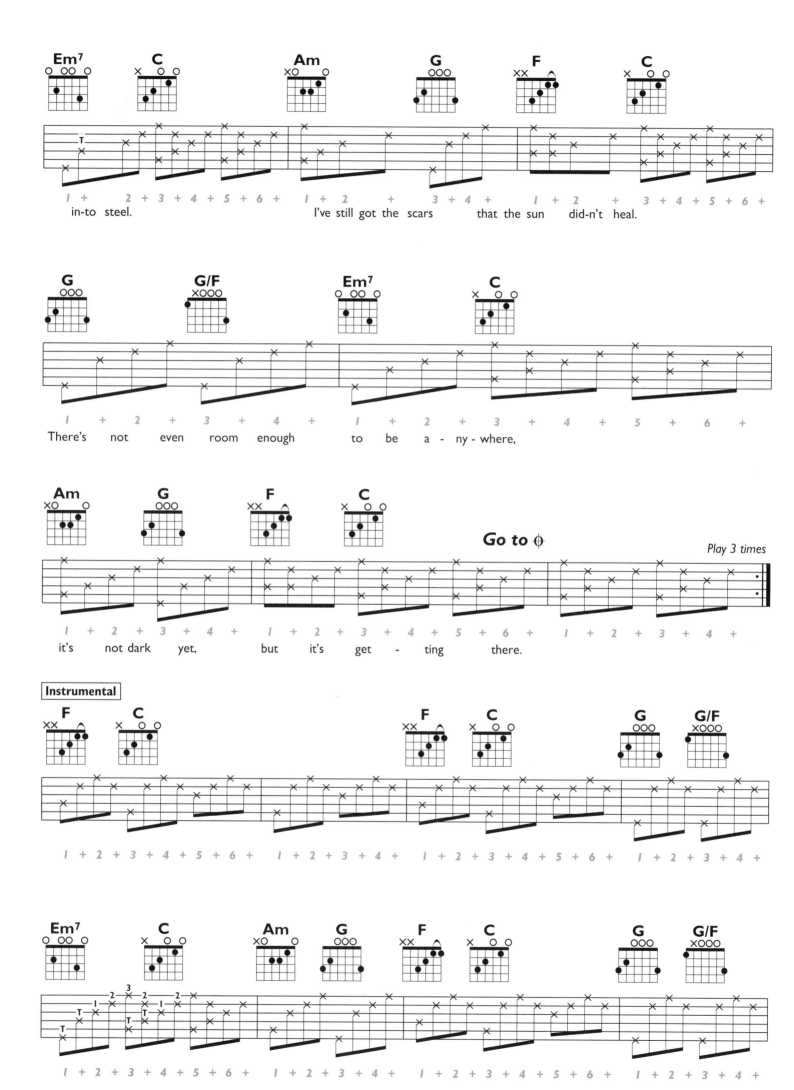

**Go back to %**

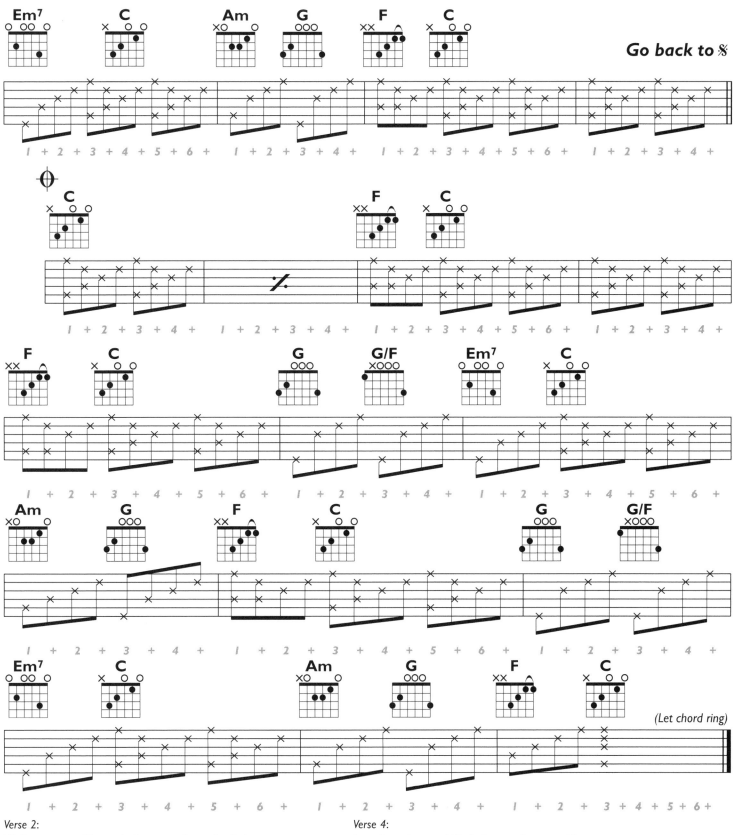

**Verse 2:**

Well my sense of humanity has gone down the drain
Behind every beautiful thing there's been some kind of pain
She wrote me a letter and she wrote it so kind
She put down in writing what was in her mind
I just don't see why I should even care
It's not dark yet, but it's getting there

**Verse 3:**

Well, I've been to London and I've been to gay Paree
I've followed the river and I got to the sea
I've been down on the bottom of a world full of lies
I ain't looking for nothing in anyone's eyes
Sometimes my burden seems more than I can bear
It's not dark yet, but it's getting there

**Verse 4:**

I was born here and I'll die here against my will
I know it looks like I'm moving, but I'm standing still
Every nerve in my body is so vacant and numb
I can't even remember what it was I came here to get away from
Don't even hear a murmur of a prayer
It's not dark yet, but it's getting there.

# ONE TOO MANY MORNINGS
## WORDS AND MUSIC BY BOB DYLAN

Try fingering a **C** chord (as on p.6) and then move to the **C/B.**

**F/A** is exactly like the **F** on p.6, with the addition of the open 5th string.

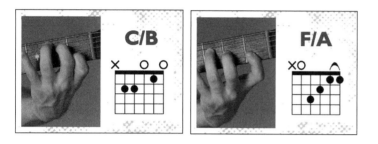

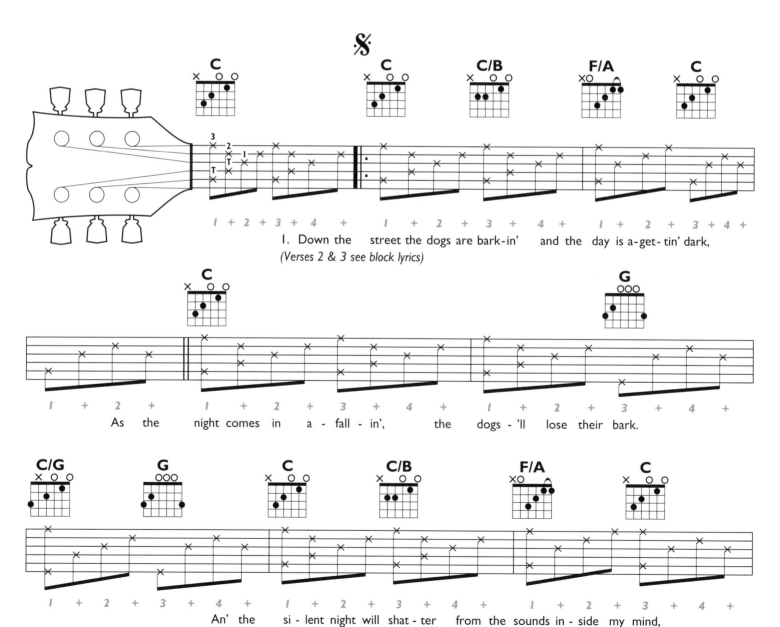

1. Down the street the dogs are bark-in' and the day is a-get-tin' dark,
*(Verses 2 & 3 see block lyrics)*

As the night comes in a-fall-in', the dogs-'ll lose their bark.

An' the si-lent night will shat-ter from the sounds in-side my mind,

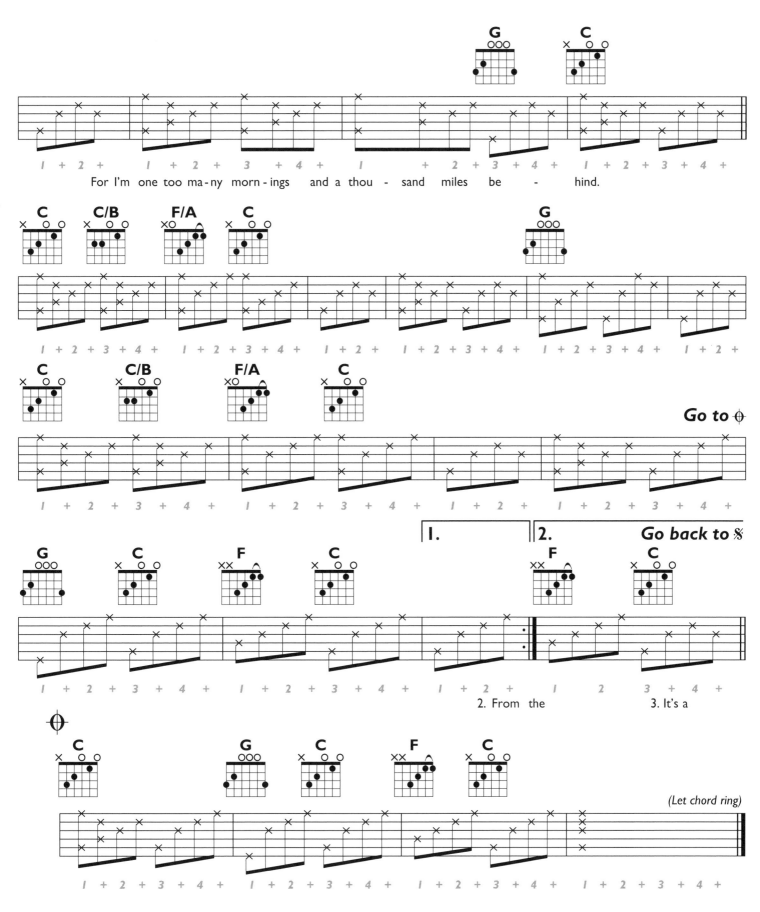

For I'm one too ma-ny morn-ings and a thou - sand miles be - hind.

Go to ⊕

1.

2.

Go back to ℅

2. From the     3. It's a

(Let chord ring)

Verse 2:
From the crossroads of my doorstep,
My eyes they start to fade,
As I turn my head back to the room
Where my love and I have laid.
An' I gaze back to the street,
The sidewalk and the sign,
And I'm one too many mornings
An' a thousand miles behind.

Verse 3:
It's a restless hungry feeling
That don't mean no one no good,
When ev'rything I'm a-sayin'
You can say it just as good.
You're right from your side,
I'm right from mine.
We're both just one too many mornings
An' a thousand miles behind.

# IT AIN'T ME, BABE
## WORDS AND MUSIC BY BOB DYLAN

Don't be put off by the chord names for this song. Start with **Am/C**. Play this by fingering a regular **Am** shape (e.g., on p.11), and then add your little finger as shown. To play **Bm/D**, simply slide your hand in this shape up two frets.

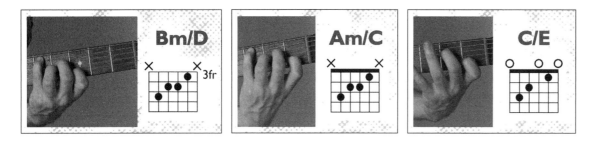

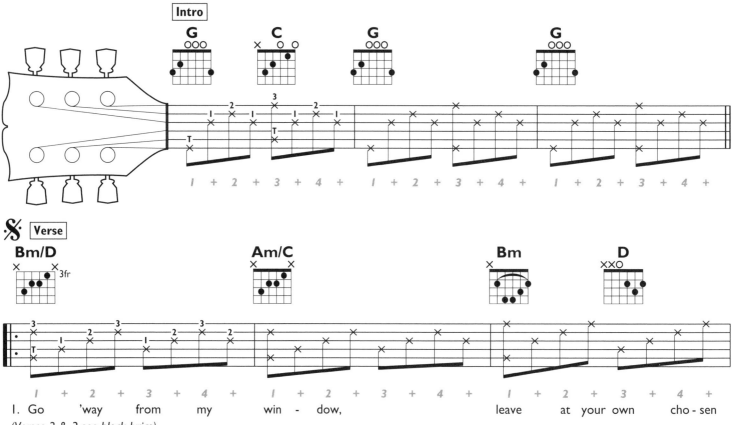

1. Go 'way from my win - dow, leave at your own cho - sen
*(Verses 2 & 3 see block lyrics)*

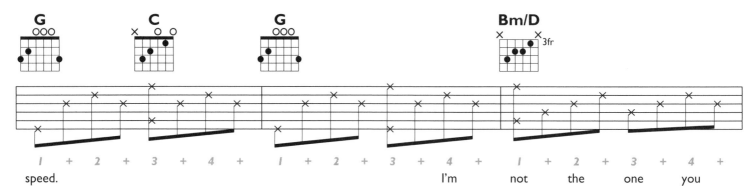

speed. I'm not the one you

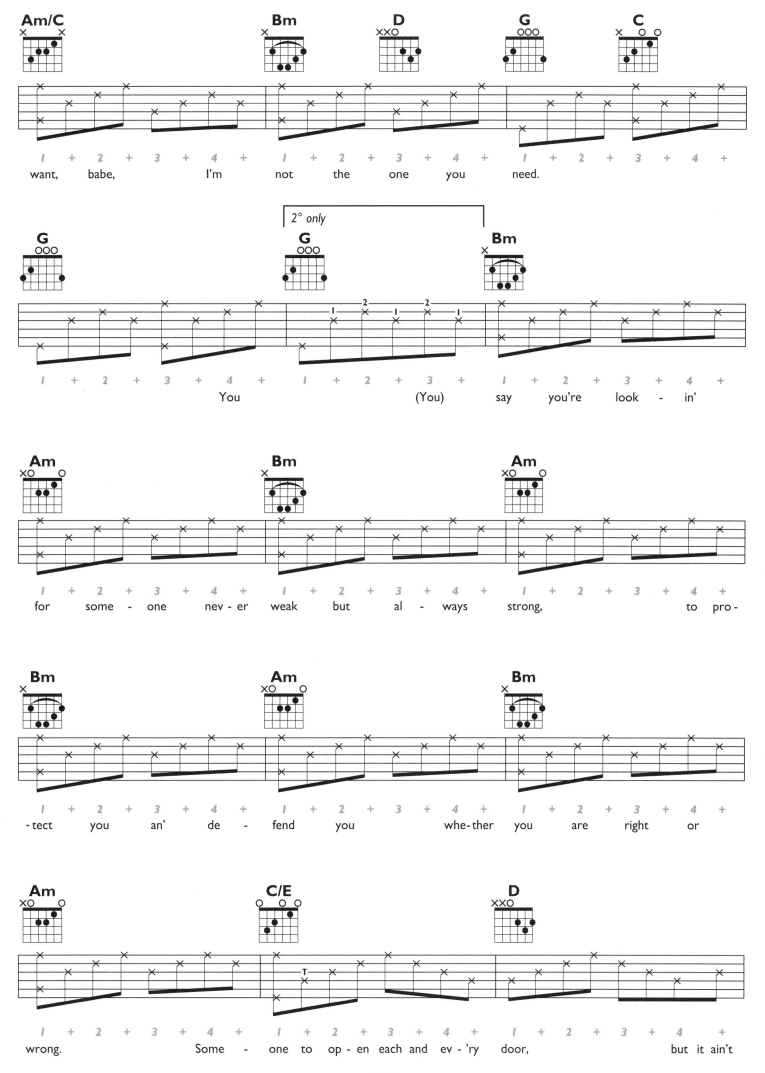

want,    babe,    I'm    not    the    one    you    need.

You    (You)    say    you're    look - in'

for    some - one    nev - er    weak    but    al - ways    strong,    to pro -

- tect    you    an'    de - fend    you    whe - ther    you    are    right    or

wrong.    Some - one    to    op - en    each    and    ev - 'ry    door,    but it ain't

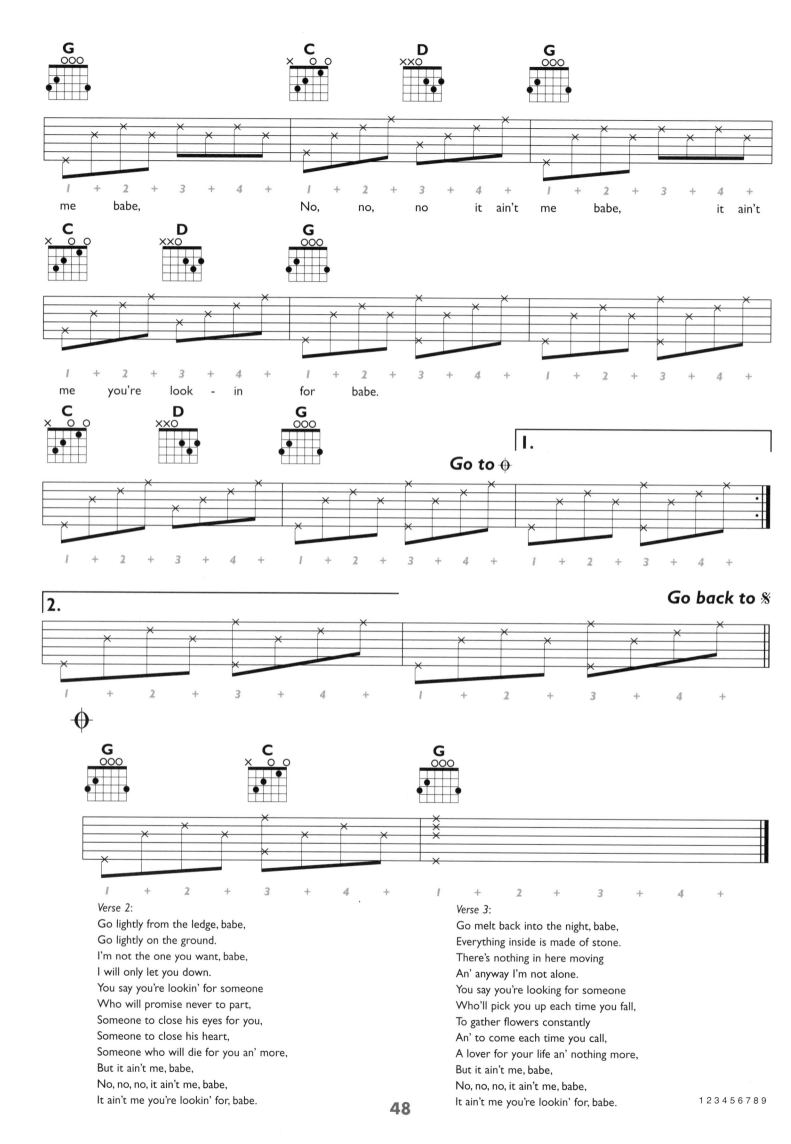

Verse 2:

Go lightly from the ledge, babe,
Go lightly on the ground.
I'm not the one you want, babe,
I will only let you down.
You say you're lookin' for someone
Who will promise never to part,
Someone to close his eyes for you,
Someone to close his heart,
Someone who will die for you an' more,
But it ain't me, babe,
No, no, no, it ain't me, babe,
It ain't me you're lookin' for, babe.

Verse 3:

Go melt back into the night, babe,
Everything inside is made of stone.
There's nothing in here moving
An' anyway I'm not alone.
You say you're looking for someone
Who'll pick you up each time you fall,
To gather flowers constantly
An' to come each time you call,
A lover for your life an' nothing more,
But it ain't me, babe,
No, no, no, it ain't me, babe,
It ain't me you're lookin' for, babe.